Eleanor Hunt.

15th September 1981.

MODGE (x 4!)

4 egg
8 oz nuts
12 oz SR flour
16 oz sugar
1lb 4 oz chopped dates
1 oz butter.

Light oven - 4 (180°C) + grease small tin. Melt butter + then add dry ingreds, followed by beaten egg. Bake 20 mins (golden/set) + cut into fingers.

OVER 200 IDEAS FOR PACKED MEALS

THE LUNCHBOX BOOK

Compiled by
June Weatherall and Elizabeth Marchetti

Designed by Sara Kidd and Royston Edwards
Illustrations by Royston Edwards
Cover photographs by Spike Powell
Recipes from Family Circle magazine kitchen

CIRCLE BOOKS

First published in 1981 by Circle Books, Elm House, Elm Street, London WC1X 0BP
Typeset by Text Filmsetters, 199 High Street, Orpington, Kent
Printed in Milan by New Interlitho

ISBN 0 907120 06 7 (Hardback)
ISBN 0 907120 09 1 (Paperback)

CONTENTS

HOW TO USE THIS BOOK

For lots of reasons – price, availability, choice, convenience – more people than ever are taking packed meals with them to school or work every day. But this means an extra chore for whoever has to prepare them – the woman (or maybe man in these liberated days) of the house, or the actual eater. This book has been designed to help the packed-meal providers by taking some of the slog out of the task. No book can help you with the actual physical work, but it can help you with some of the thought involved in planning, preparation, packing and most important, give you ideas for nourishing, varied and interesting meals.

On the next few pages you'll find general suggestions on planning, preparing, packaging and convenience foods, then you'll come to the person-by-person, season-by-season and day-by-day section. Here's how this works.

Types of people

The main groups of packed meal consumers are men and women at work, school children, and slimmers, so the book is divided into these three sections. Obviously you can switch from one section to another – a school child might like a slightly smaller version of an adult menu, men and women at work might fancy some of the food suggested in the slimmer's section.

Men and women at work

They need nourishing food to revive them and help them work effectively in the afternoon. The sort of work they do will alter their needs. Someone who works manually in the open air will need more in the way of stocking up than a sedentary office worker. Add or subtract from the menus as suggested for school children.

School children

All young people are growing and need the right kind of food at lunchtime to help them do this. But school children vary in age from four/five to eighteen and the amount they want to eat will vary greatly. Rather than make arbitrary age divisions (which wouldn't account for appetite anyway), they are included under one heading. If the menu seems too large for a five-year-old or too small for a strapping sixteen then subtract from or add to it, bearing in mind the nutrient chart on page 9.

Slimmers

It's a sad fact of life that no food will make a person slimmer – but a packed meal where calories are counted could prevent them from becoming any fatter. The menus in this section are for interesting, tasty meals containing enough calories, but not too many.

Season by season

What you want to eat varies according to the time of year and certain foods are more available, and cheaper, at certain seasons, too. So it makes sense to divide the book into spring, summer, autumn and winter. But, of course, there's no need to stick rigidly to these sections – after all the temperature on many a supposedly

summer's day would be more normal in November!

Menus

Under each of the four seasonal sections there are twenty menus for both men and women at work and school children and ten for slimmers – five a page to give a balanced and interesting week's meals. The menus include a balanced mixture of home-cooked and convenience foods. If you're going to have a busy day on Monday and Tuesday's menu contains something you just won't have time to cook, then swap the days about. If you've bought a supply of ham because it was on special offer, and ham doesn't appear on the menu, then substitute it for something else in the same range of nourishment value – see the chart on page 9. Personal choice will play a part too – not everyone likes everything. The menus and their contents can be shuffled around like a pack of cards to give you innumerable combinations. But remember to always aim for a balanced meal containing all the nutrients required. The items with a black star mean the recipe is on the facing page. Those with a white star are fully explained in the daily notes.

The recipes

The recipes aren't for ordinary items that you will already know how to cook or that you can find easily in your cookbooks, but for slightly 'unusual' things that are good for packed lunches – and for other meals eaten at home, too.

Daily notes

These give suggestions for how you can vary the menus to suit tastes, use up bulk-bought foods, substitute a convenience item for a home-made one, use up leftovers, ideas for drinks, and tips for packing and reminders like 'pack a spoon' if yogurt, for instance, is included in the menu.

Drinks

Drinks have not been included with the menus. They are so much a matter of both taste and availability. Many packed meal consumers are perfectly happy with their flasks of tea or coffee every day throughout the year. But drinks haven't been forgotten, they are a vital part of a packed meal, and there is a section devoted entirely to them, see page 102.

Special Centre Section – Packed meals for leisure days

Cost and convenience are two reasons why families, or friends, out together for the day – whether visiting relations or friends, or going to the sea or countryside, on a birthday treat expedition – now take their food with them. Firstly this section includes movable feasts, that is where food is eaten on the move, perhaps in public transport or in a public place, so it must be especially non-messy. There are family and friends picnic lunches for a day out as well as menus for special occasion picnics, where the food and its presentation has a luxury (though not over-expensive) touch. Finally suggestions for barbeques and children's party picnics.

PLANNING AND PREPARATION

Nutrition and balance
The first two things you should ask yourself when you're thinking about packed meals are: is the food itself nutritious and is the meal as a whole balanced? After all, the portable meal you're providing, for others or yourself, is the half-time reviver to enable the eater to go back to work re-nourished and full of energy. A stodgy meal may fill you up between breakfast and supper, but you'll probably spend the afternoon wanting to doze, not to mention putting on weight.

Easy to eat
All packed meals should be easy to eat in the surroundings where they are going to be consumed. For instance, school lunches for younger children should be extra easy, the adults in charge won't want to spend ages afterwards wiping down faces, chairs, tables, maybe even walls.

An adult at work may be able to keep a small supply of cutlery, plates, paper towels etc handy to cope with slightly more complicated items like, say, dips. A special adults-only picnic can come complete with all the right eating utensils so more complicated foods can be served.

Below is a quick reference list of really easy-to-eat food that's perfect for individual portions, too.

Hard-boiled eggs, Cheese wedges, Sausages, Apples, Pears, Peeled oranges in segments, Plums, Bananas, Dried fruit such as apricots, sultanas, currants and raisins, Tomatoes, Cucumber chunks, Celery sticks, Raw carrots, Scones, Plain small cakes and biscuits, like flapjacks, shortbread, Handful of muesli or crunchy oat cereal.

Adding interest
Packed meals should be interesting and enjoyable to eat. Banish boredom by making them colourful when you can, just a touch of a brightly-coloured vegetable, fruit or even chutney can make all the difference. And think about textures too. A meal containing all 'soft' food is dreary, one containing nothing but hard-to-chew 'crunch' would be equally bad. Aim for a good mixture. Flavour, too, should be mixed: avoid an all-spicy, or all-bland, menu too.

Saving time
It saves shopping and cooking time, fuel as well, if you do a tandem operation by thinking – and cooking – packed meals and home meals together. Here's how: (take heart, it's easy once you get the hang of it, and once you start, you'll think of lots of ideas for yourself).

★ Having boiled eggs for breakfast? If so pop a few extra into the water and leave them to hard-boil. Use as they are or cut up for egg roll or sandwich fillings, or salads.

★ Buy a larger chicken or joint of meat than you need and use the surplus for packed meals. Or buy an extra chicken or chicken parts and roast with the main one. Use for fillings or as they are.

★ Buy and cook extra sausages, use as above.

★ Making a meat loaf, pasties, quiche, pie or flan? Then cook one or two extra individual portions and store in your fridge or freezer.

★ Prepare extra salad and put some aside, without dressing, if lettuce is involved, in the fridge. This way they keep for several days.

★ Wash, prepare and peel extra vegetables. Cook potatoes and save them cooked (for salads and fillings), save carrots, celery etc uncooked. Children love munching them and they help care for teeth if eaten after rolls, cake or biscuits.

★ Having trifle, fruit crumble, fruit pie or tart for pudding? Then make an extra large one, or one or two individual ones. Keep in your fridge or freezer.

★ Batch baking makes sense too, if you have a freezer.

Planning to suit yourself
Pre-planning – whether on paper or in your head – is essential for the lunchbox provider. Not just for time-saving and peace of mind, but because shops tend not to be open first thing in the morning and many a school bus or train has been missed while the bread is being buttered or the sandwich packed.

But if you're not one of the perfect plan-ahead types – with a freezer full of ready-packed goodies – don't feel obliged to emulate them. Work out the system that suits you and your life style best. The ideas below may help you to work out a method.

Day by day
Perhaps night by night would be more accurate. If you possibly can, it does pay to make up lunch packs the previous evening – they will keep fresh in the fridge. For this method of planning the 'must-remembers' are to make sure you have sufficient bread, rolls, crispbread, fruit and a portable drink.

As your basic standby, use

the saving-something-from-supper technique suggested in 'Saving time' above. Filled sandwiches or rolls should keep for two days in the fridge. Salads packed in seal-top containers will also survive well for several days in the fridge.

Below are some ingredients you could save from a main meal. Chopped up, or grated, two or three can be mixed together.

Diced cucumber, Chopped celery, Grated carrots, Chopped green peppers, Tomato wedges, Cold, boiled potatoes, Shredded raw cabbage, Canned fish, Chopped nuts, Cooked meat slices, Grated cheese, Slices of sausage.

With the addition of fruit, a drink and the odd goody, it should be possible to make a balanced packed meal a quick-to-do assembly job. A good standby is to have a jar or tin of pâté, paste, yeast extract, cheese spread, peanut butter (or whatever the eater's favourite is) on hand as an emergency roll, or sandwich filler.

Week by week

If you have a freezer and if the eater (or eaters) can be persuaded that a little repetition (of nourishing, well-balanced food, of course) is no bad thing – it makes sense to do a batch preparation.

For one week buy, say, a roll a day per person and/or enough bread and make or buy a quantity of two or three fillings. Make up suitable amounts for one helping, pack individually in small freezer bags and freeze.

Home-made or bought pasties, quiches, pies of all kinds can be added to the individual freezer packs. While fresh fruit, yogurts, salads, tomatoes and celery – the 'balancing' items – can make variety.

A month at a time

This sounds horrendous – but it's not. You don't have to cook and prepare a month's supply in one go. The principle is preparing by batch, by tem – and then freezing them. For example, if you're baking, make say, a quiche, when it's cooked and cool, cut and pack in individual portions and freeze. When cooking cakes, sausage rolls, biscuits, put aside some specially and freeze. Use a glut of apples, or other good-freezing fruit, to make into pies and crumbles and cook and freeze them in small foil containers.

If cheese, salami or anything else suitable, is on special offer at the supermarket, buy in bulk to make into fillings. Then arm yourself with softened (it goes further) butter or margarine and a supply of bread and/or rolls and start spreading. A note of warning, egg mayonnaise, and salad fillings do not freeze well. Good freezers are cheese, fish, and cooked meats. When lunch packs are needed an assortment of items can be put together, a few fresh ones added for balance, if necessary, and hey presto!

Nutrient	Purpose	Sources suitable for packed meals
Proteins	For growth and repair of body tissue	Cheese, meat (including pastes), egg, fish (including pastes and canned fish), bread. Cheese is a very rich source
Fat	For energy	Butter, margarine, bacon, cheese
Vitamin A	For aiding growth, vision. For protecting moist tissues	Butter, carrots, margarine, liver
Vitamin B	For helping body to convert food to usable material	Most protein sources and bread
Vitamin C	For keeping skin clear and preventing scurvy	Vegetables and citrus fruits
Vitamin D	For helping bone development	Canned fish, butter, margarine and eggs
Carbohydrates	For providing energy	Bread and cakes

PACKAGING

Good packaging can make all the difference between a packed meal that looks appetizing and easy to eat and one that looks unpleasant with crushed pastry, fallen-apart sandwiches and squashed tomatoes! Here are some tips on packaging – that all important ingredient of packed meals.

Plastic containers

With lids that seal firmly these now come in attractive colours, and can be bought in a wide range of sizes and shapes. Chain stores, supermarkets and firms like Tupperware can supply ones to suit every requirement. Easy to clean and almost indestructible, they are a good investment for anyone who has to prepare packed meals.

Small squat cylindrical containers are excellent for any kind of 'soft' puddings like yogurt, mousses, fruit salads, fresh soft fruit and so on. Fairly flat square or rectangular ones are good for sandwiches and for rolls or French bread, slightly deeper ones are available. The long, narrow shallow kind, often sold for rashers of bacon are good for celery sticks and salads.

Don't forget too, to invest in a few small containers for things like butter, sugar, salad dressings and seasonings. And good well-sealing ones for milk and drinks are essential too.

Do a little shopping around, visit a chain store, ironmongers or supermarket and decide which you think will be most suitable for your needs. If you are preparing packed meals for two, or even three people, invest in a colour code – have a special set of different coloured containers for each person. In this way you'll avoid the situation when A takes B's ham sandwiches. And A likes mustard and B loathes it!

As you don't want to lose your containers, and children at school are often somewhat casual about their belongings, it makes sense to have the child's name or initials on them. Paint them on the outside with nail varnish.

Although you may find yourself spending a few pounds on containers like these – say a week or two's school dinner money – they're worth it in the long run. For even if a time does come when you're no longer a packed meal preparer, they'll still be useful as general cupboard and fridge containers.

Secondhand containers

Many bought foods these days come in containers which can be used again. Cream, ready-prepared salads, cream cheeses, margarine and so on are often sold in plastic tubs with lids. These are extremely useful for packing all kinds of food like milk jellies (make them in the containers), salads, soft fruit, little cakes, biscuits etc. Don't forget though, that the lids of these kinds of containers are often not so well fitting, nor is the plastic so strong, as that of the bought plastic containers mentioned above, so treat them gently.

Large square or oblong containers that have held margarine or ice-cream for the freezer can be used as complete lunch-boxes with rolls, fruit, cake and

so on separately wrapped inside them.

The rigid tinfoil containers with lids in which you buy Chinese take-away meals are also useful. You can cook individual fruit crumbles in them, pop on the lid when they're cool.

Some 'own brands' of golden syrup are now sold in rigid transparent containers with screw-on lids. These make good cold pud containers. And marmalade is sometimes sold in tins with a plastic lid. These make sensible mini biscuit or cake tins. But make sure the edges where the tin lid has been cut off are quite smooth. Even the smallest piece of metal can result in a nasty cut.

Bought individual pies are often packed in rigid tinfoil containers, wrapped up inside a cardboard outer box. Save the tinfoil containers and box. Cook individual pies in the containers, wrap them and reinsert in the cardboard box. If the pies survived uncrushed packed like this from the factory, to the shop, to your home – the chances are that they'll survive the journey to work or school too.

Save plastic bags from bread as well – see under 'plastic' bags for how to use them.

So save all your containers – you never know when they'll come in useful.

Vacuum flasks

These too can be bought in a wide variety of shapes and sizes to suit all needs. Use small or large conventional pouring ones for hot drinks and soups that don't contain large pieces of meat or vegetables. If possible pack the milk and sugar separately for tea – it tastes better that way. Where soup is recommended in the menus, a cup hasn't been mentioned in the 'pack' section – it's simpler to use the cup on the flask. But if the consumer prefers to eat their soup rather than drink it, then pack a separate bowl, or mug, and spoon.

Wide-necked vacuum flasks open a whole new world to the packed meal preparer as thick nourishing soups with chunks of meat and vegetables, and hot dishes like stews, can be kept warm in them. You can eat straight out of the flask, or take a bowl and spoon or fork.

Don't forget either that on a hot day you can keep drinks extra cool with pieces of ice in a vacuum flask

Some schools aren't too happy about small children taking conventional vacuum flasks with them. If they're dropped, the glass inside can shatter and that's not a nice thought. There are now unbreakable flasks, specially made for children, on the market. So if you have a young school child – look out for this type in the shops.

Cling film

This thin, transparent wrapping material is a boon. Wrapped in it, rolls and sandwiches, pies, cakes, tomatoes etc stay fresh and tidy. And afterwards it can be screwed up into a small easily-disposable ball. It's especially useful for keeping several items separate from each other in one container. A nicely-laid out salad on a paper plate covered with cling film is an attractive quick and simple way of packaging.

PACKAGING

Many people find cling film fiddly and exasperating to cut from a roll – but it's much easier if you have a dispenser. So look out for one.

Tinfoil

Tinfoil on a roll can be used in much the same way as cling film, but it does have an extra advantage. Because it is more rigid it is better for packing more fragile items like pieces of quiche.

Rigid tinfoil containers, often sold for freezers are also extremely useful. Those with lids can be used for packing all kinds of foods.

Plastic bags

The most economical way to buy these is on a roll. Small ones are good for individual rolls and sandwiches, larger ones can take several items like say, bananas and apples. They're also useful for putting peel or biscuit wrappings in to throw away in a refuse bin at work or school, or to bring rubbish back home for disposal.

For safety's sake don't send small children to school with a head-sized plastic bag, unless it's well perforated – keep to smaller ones.

If you're going to batch prepare meals and store them in the freezer, you'll need the tougher freezer type bags. Otherwise if one of the thinner ones bursts you could be discovering sandwiches in all the odd corners of your freezer.

Paper and paper bags

Greaseproof paper has its place in the packed meal scene. It is perfectly good for wrapping pieces of cake, pies etc. Elastic bands are the best method to keep it together. And the good old paper bag should not be scorned as a container for fruit, or an extra protective covering for other foods already wrapped in cling film or greaseproof paper.

Drinking utensils

A plastic beaker with a well-sealed lid is essential for home-made fruit or milky drinks. Here it's essential to have a really good one – if not the results can be disastrous.

Apart from the above, cups and beakers don't play a very large part in individual packed meals. The cup from the top of a vacuum flask can be used for hot drinks, and cold drinks in cartons or cans are better and less messy drunk with a straw. Of course, for family picnics, disposable or plastic cups or beakers, one for each person, are necessary.

Plates

For school children these aren't really necessary – eating straight from a container is easier or the lid of a container can be a plate substitute. But for adults who perhaps want to make more of an occasion of a meal, it does make sense to put all the ingredients out on a plate. If you have the facilities at work it's a good idea to keep a plate in the office and wash it after use. Paper plates are useful as they can be thrown away after use and save the bother of bringing dirty dishes home.

Cutlery

Plastic cutlery is a good buy for packed meals. It's light to carry and if it gets lost it won't break the bank, or anyone's heart. Some people complain that plastic knives are useless. If food is that difficult to cut, then it makes sense to cut it at home first anyway.

Napkins

Pieces of paper towel make very efficient napkins for spreading on the desk top before you start, protecting your clothes and for wiping your hands. Man-sized tissue handkerchiefs are good too. Look out for special offers of proper paper napkins too. In July you can often buy holly decorated ones quite cheaply or birthday or golden wedding ones with designs that just didn't sell.

Lunchboxes

A lunchbox which will take all the ingredients of a meal makes sense. And many manufacturers realising this have produced some very attractive ones. Tupperware, for instance, do a good one especially for children. The metal one photographed on the cover of this book will hold everything needed. And if the consumer doesn't mind going without a handle, then a plastic container in a large size would do.

But don't go dashing out and buy a container without considering a few things first. For a child at primary school, a lunchbox is a very good idea, and fun to have as well. But for an older youngster who is carrying a lot of books, games kit and maybe a musical instrument, a complete lunchbox would be an uncarriable burden. Much better to pack their meal in small containers that can slot into gaps between books in a bag or case. The same goes for adults with a long journey to work by public transport. Many an executive briefcase holds several bags of edible goodies! But for someone travelling to work by car, on the other hand, a lunchbox is probably quite acceptable.

CONVENIENCE FOODS

If you scan the supermarket shelves, grocers' and butchers' shops, freezers in freezer shops, you'll find all kinds of nutritious and time-saving items to add variety to packed meals. Here are just a few.

Cooked meats

These can be used for sandwich and roll fillings, on their own, or mixed, or even wrapped round cream cheese.

Ham
Corned beef
Haslet
Frankfurters
Salami
Liver sausage
Luncheon meats
Sliced cooked meat
Breakfast sausages
Frozen beefburgers (cooked and chopped for kebabs)

Savoury pies, pasties and ready-mades

Just add some salad or vegetables and you've the basis of a packed meal.

Scotch eggs
Ham, cheese, mushroom flans
Pork pies of all sizes
Veal and ham pies
Sausage rolls
Cornish pasties
Chicken or cheese pasties

Spreads

Keep a supply of these in your store cupboard, fridge or freezer, whichever is suitable.

Meat or fish pâtés
Tubs of cream or cottage cheese (plain or with chives, pineapple and so on)
Tubes of cream cheese, fish-flavoured spreads
Packets of cream cheese
Fish and meat pastes
Peanut butter
Jars of yeast or meat extract
Jars of other savoury spreads

Ready-to-eat or easy-to-prepare vegetables

Buy individual containers, or a larger one and decant a suitable amount from the fridge each day into a plastic container. Add mayonnaise or dressing if necessary.

Tubs of coleslaw
Tubs of mixed salad
Tubs of potato salad
Cans of mixed vegetables or potato salad
Cans of baked beans, sweetcorn, peas, new potatoes etc
Frozen packs of peas, beans, mixed vegetables

Puddings

These go right across the range from dairy products to pies, cakes and tarts.

Yogurt
Individual mousses
Individual trifles
Large or small fruit pies
Jam tarts
Mince pies
Large or small treacle tarts
Cup cakes
Mini Swiss rolls
Packets of shortbread

Treats

Most children, and plenty of adults, like a little 'treat' included in their lunchbox. Here are just some

Chocolate-covered biscuits
Chocolate-covered nuts and raisins
Chocolate bars of all kinds
Packets of nuts
Packets of savouries: crisps, potato sticks, Twiglets etc

MEN AND WOMEN AT WORK

Monday

☆ Cheesy corn rolls

Blackcurrant mousse

Fresh fruit

Tuesday

☆ Chicken vegetable salad

☆ Fruit Whip Flan

Wednesday

★ Chicory Nicoise

Wholemeal roll and butter

Chocolate cake

Thursday

☆ Tasty Turkey Spread rolls

Celery sticks

☆ Orange salad

★ *see recipe opposite*
☆ *see daily notes*

Friday

☆ Celery and tuna double deckers

Red cabbage salad

★ Cherry Franzipan Flan

Cherry Franzipan Flan

Monday

For the rolls spread corn relish over the grated or sliced cheese. Use leftover Sunday pud or a bought mousse. **Pack:** spoon. **For tomorrow:** cook a piece of chicken. Have some cold cooked veg – carrots, peas etc – for the salad. Make Fruit Whip Flan, see page 23.

Tuesday

Add mayonnaise to the diced, cooked veg. **Pack:** knife, fork and spoon. **For tomorrow:** buy and prepare the ingredients for Chicory Nicoise. Make or buy a large chocolate cake or some small ones.

Wednesday

Assemble Chicory Nicoise. **Pack:** knife and fork. **For tomorrow:** make Tasty Turkey Spread, see page 23, or buy some turkey pâté. Peel and segment a mixture of oranges, tangerines, satsumas etc., whatever you have, for the orange salad.

Thursday

Fill the rolls. Sprinkle the orange salad with sugar if necessary. **Pack:** spoon. **For tomorrow:** flake canned tuna and chop celery. Slice red cabbage. Make Cherry Franzipan Flan.

Friday

Make double decker sandwiches, see page 41. Add dressing to red cabbage, and a few currants or sultanas if liked. **Pack:** 2 forks.

Chicory Nicoise

Take the French dressing in a separate jar and pour over the salad just before eating.

For 4 portions

4 slices bread from a large loaf
3 tablespoons oil
1 (1¾ oz, 50 g) can anchovies
4 oz (100 g) garlic sausage
2 tomatoes
2 hard-boiled eggs
8 stuffed olives
2 tablespoons chopped parsley
4 chicons
French dressing

1. Remove crusts from the bread and cut the bread into ½ in cubes. Heat the oil in a large pan, add bread cubes and fry on all sides until golden brown. Drain on kitchen paper.
2. Drain oil from anchovies, chop garlic sausage, cut tomatoes and hard-boiled eggs into quarters. Place in a large bowl and add olives and parsley. Mix well.
3. Wash the chicory, trim base and outside leaves. Cut into slices and add to a large bowl with the bread cubes.

Cherry Franzipan Flan

Adding bought marzipan to a flan gives a delicious flavour and chewy texture. You will find it keeps well for at least a week if wrapped in foil. Alternatively, store in the freezer.

For 6 to 8 portions

Quick mix pastry:
6 oz (150 g) plain flour
3 oz (75 g) soft margarine
1 oz (25 g) castor sugar
1 egg

Filling
4 oz (100 g) soft margarine
4 oz (100 g) castor sugar
1 egg
3 oz (75 g) semolina
2 oz (50 g) glacé cherries
2 oz (50 g) seedless raisins
4 oz (100 g) marzipan
Icing sugar

1. Place an 8 in fluted flan ring on a baking sheet.
2. Place the flour, margarine, sugar and egg in a bowl. Mix together with a fork to form a firm dough. Turn out on to a lightly-floured surface; knead dough until smooth.
3. Roll out pastry to a circle 1½ in larger than flan ring. Line the flan ring. Chill the pastry for 20 minutes.
4. Prepare a moderately hot oven (400°F, 200°C, Gas Mark 6).
5. Place the margarine, castor sugar, egg and semolina in a bowl. Beat with a wooden spoon until smooth and creamy; cut the cherries into quarters and add to the bowl with the raisins. Roughly chop the marzipan and fold it into the mixture with a metal spoon.
6. Spread the mixture in pastry flan case, level with the back of metal spoon. Bake in centre of oven for 20 minutes. Reduce oven temperature to moderate (350°F, 180°C, Gas Mark 4) and continue cooking for 20 to 25 minutes until filling is set and well browned.
7. Leave to cool in ring 5 minutes, then remove ring and slide flan on to a cooling rack. When cold, sprinkle liberally with sifted icing sugar.

MEN AND WOMEN AT WORK

Monday

Meat and pickle baps

☆ Egg mayonnaise

Fresh fruit

Tuesday

★ Jamaica Patties

Celery sticks

Chocolate mousse

Wednesday

☆ Cheese and Onion Roll

Apple Crumble

Thursday

Pork pie

Coleslaw

Wholemeal roll and butter

☆ Rhubarb Ripple

★ see recipe opposite
☆ see daily notes

Friday

Chunks of cheese

★ Oaten Biscuits and butter

Orange and banana salad

Fruit and nut chocolate

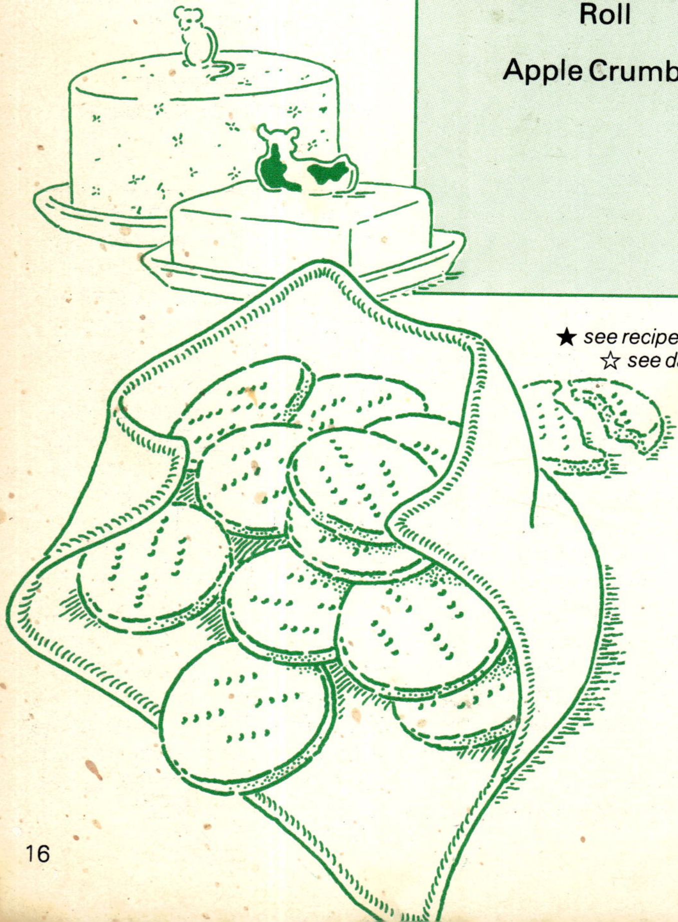

Oaten Biscuits

Monday

Use Sunday joint leftovers, or canned or bought luncheon meat with a favourite pickle for the baps. For egg mayonnaise, hard boil two eggs, cool in cold water, shell and chop. Then add seasoning and enough mayonnaise to mix. A few chopped chives make it specially tasty. Pack in a small container. **Pack:** fork. **For tomorrow:** make Jamaica Patties. Prepare celery. Make or buy chocolate mousse.

Tuesday

Pack: spoon. **For tomorrow:** make Cheese and Onion Roll, see page 25. Make the apple crumble.

Wednesday

Pack: knife and two forks. **For tomorrow:** make or buy pork pie. Make Rhubarb Ripple, see page 25.

Thursday

Cut pork pie into pieces for easy eating. **Pack:** fork and spoon. **For tomorrow:** make Oaten Biscuits. Peel and segment oranges for salad, put in a container, sprinkle with soft brown sugar and store in the fridge.

Friday

Pack Oaten Biscuits in an airtight container. Cut chunks of cheese and pack separately. Add sliced bananas to oranges. Pack butter separately in a small container. **Pack:** knife and spoon.

Jamaica Patties

Curried vegetables in an easy-to-eat patty make a tasty meal that's convenient to pack.

Makes 8

Filling:

1 medium-sized onion
2 medium-sized carrots
1 medium-sized potato
1 tablespoon cooking oil
2 level teaspoons curry powder
½ level teaspoon chilli seasoning
1 small (7.94 oz, 225 g) can baked beans in tomato sauce
1 tablespoon lemon juice
1 oz (25 g) sultanas
½ level teaspoon salt

Pastry:

8 oz (200 g) plain flour
½ level teaspoon ground turmeric
½ level teaspoon salt
3 oz (75 g) margarine
5 tablespoons milk and water, mixed
Oil for shallow frying

1. Peel the onion and chop finely. Peel the carrots and potato and grate coarsely.
2. Heat 1 tablespoon oil in a saucepan. Add the onion and fry gently for about 5 minutes, until softened. Add carrots, potato, curry powder and chilli and cook for a further 5 minutes. Add remaining filling ingredients and 2 tablespoons water and cook gently for 10 minutes. Leave to cool.
3. Sift flour, turmeric and salt into a mixing bowl. Place the margarine and milk and water mixture into a small saucepan and heat until margarine has melted. Pour on to flour and mix to a soft dough with a fork.
4. Turn out on to a floured board and knead with fingertips.
5. Roll out thinly and cut into eight 6 in rounds. Divide filling between rounds, placing a little in the centre of each. Brush edges of pastry with water and fold over, pinching edges together to seal. Chill.
6. Heat about ½ in depth of oil or cooking fat in a large frying pan. Fry patties, a few at a time until deep golden brown on both sides, about 5 minutes. Drain on kitchen paper.

Oaten Biscuits

A crumbly oatmeal biscuit, delicious with cheese. Store them in a tin.

Makes 18 to 20 biscuits

4 oz (100 g) self-raising flour
4 oz (100 g) medium oatmeal
¼ level teaspoon salt
3 oz (75 g) margarine
1 level teaspoon sugar
½ level teaspoon bicarbonate of soda
1 egg

1. Prepare a moderate oven (350°F, 180°C, Gas Mark 4). Brush a baking sheet with oil.
2. Place flour, oatmeal and salt into a bowl. Add the margarine and rub in until the mixture resembles fine breadcrumbs.
3. Stir in the sugar and bicarbonate of soda. Beat the egg and mix in to form a stiff dough.
4. Turn out on to a floured surface and knead lightly until smooth. Roll out to ¼ in thickness and cut into rounds with a 2½ in plain cutter. Place on the baking sheet and prick rounds with a fork. Knead trimmings together; re-roll and repeat.
5. Bake in centre of oven for 20 to 25 minutes or until biscuits are pale golden brown. Leave to cool on a wire rack.

MEN AND WOMEN AT WORK

Monday

Tomato soup

Cold meat and onion rolls

Fruit crumble

Tuesday

☆ Continental Flan

Cream cheese filled finger rolls

Stewed fruit

Wednesday

★ Frankfurter Cabbage Salad

Wholemeal roll and butter

Chocolate mousse

Thursday

☆ Green egg baps

Mini pork pie

★ Apricot and Almond Tricorns

Friday

Fishy celery sandwiches

Fresh fruit

☆ Nut Crunch Cookies

★ see recipe opposite
☆ see daily notes

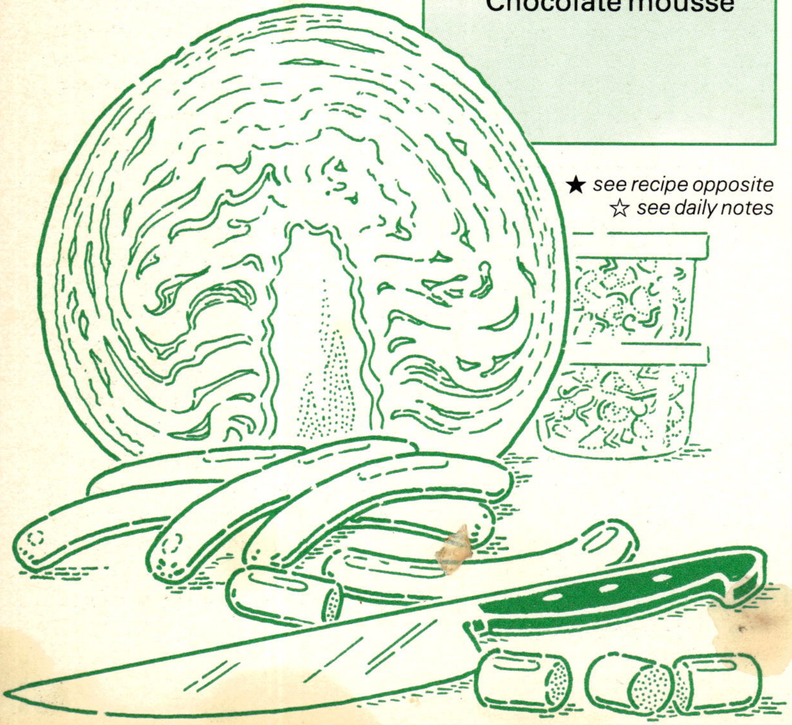

Frankfurter Cabbage Salad

Monday

Pour heated home-made or bought soup into a vacuum flask. Use slices of leftover Sunday joint and finely chopped onion (or a favourite pickle) for the rolls. If you've no fruit crumble, supply fresh fruit instead. **Pack:** spoon. **For tomorrow:** make Continental Flan, see page 27. Stew fruit.

Tuesday

Fill finger rolls with cream cheese. Sprinkle sugar on stewed fruit, if necessary, or take a small container of sugar separately. **Pack:** knife, fork and spoon. **For tomorrow:** make Frankfurter Cabbage Salad. Make or buy mousse.

Wednesday

Butter the wholemeal roll and sandwich together again. **Pack:** fork and spoon. **For tomorrow:** hard boil eggs for baps. Buy or make mini pork pie. Make Apricot and Almond Tricorns.

Thursday

Chop hard-boiled eggs. Mix with chopped cress (or watercress) and a little mayonnaise and seasoning. **Pack:** knife and fork. **For tomorrow:** flake some canned tuna and mix with chopped celery for the sandwiches. Make Nut Crunch Cookies, see page 27.

Friday

Pack: a knife if it's needed – for the fruit.

Frankfurter Cabbage Salad

This nourishing and tasty salad will keep a few days in the fridge. Pack individual portions as required.

For 4 portions

2 eggs
8 oz (200 g) white cabbage
2 carrots
1 medium-sized eating apple
2 sticks of celery
10 frankfurter sausages
4 rounded tablespoons salad cream

1. Hard boil eggs for 10 minutes; crack and leave to cool in cold water. Shell and dry on kitchen paper. Chop finely; place in a bowl.
2. Using a sharp knife, cut cabbage into fine shreds; add to the bowl.
3. Peel the carrots; grate coarsely into bowl. Quarter, core and chop apple finely; wash and chop celery, then add, with apple, to bowl.
4. Cut each frankfurter into ½ in pieces; add to bowl, with salad cream and stir well.

Apricot and Almond Tricorns

These little pastries are moist and filling. They can also be served with cream or custard for a delicious pudding.

Makes 8 to 10

Pastry:
8 oz (200 g) plain flour
1 oz (25 g) ground almonds
½ level teaspoon mixed spice
5 oz (125 g) butter
1 oz (25 g) castor sugar
1 egg yolk

Filling:
1 large (14½ oz, 411 g) can apricot halves
1 oz (25 g) flaked almonds
1 egg white
2 level tablespoons castor sugar

1. Prepare a moderately hot oven (400°F, 200°C, Gas Mark 6).
2. Place the flour, ground almonds and spice in a bowl. Add the butter and rub in until the mixture resembles fine breadcrumbs. Add 1 oz (25 g) sugar.
3. Mix the egg yolk with 1 tablespoon water. Add to bowl and mix with a fork to form a firm dough.
4. Turn out on to a floured board and knead lightly. Wrap in cling film or greaseproof paper and chill while making the filling.
5. Drain the apricots and dry on kitchen paper. Chop roughly and place in a bowl with flaked almonds; mix together.
6. Roll out the pastry and cut into 6 in rounds using a saucer as a guide. Gather together trimmings, roll out and cut out more rounds to make between 8 and 10 rounds in all.
7. Divide the filling equally between rounds, piling mixture into the centre of each. Brush edges of pastry with water and fold three edges into the centre to form a triangle, pinching the edges together to seal them.
8. Place tricorns on a baking sheet. Beat together egg white and sugar with a fork and brush over the pastry. Make small balls with pastry trimmings and place in the centre of each tricorn to decorate; brush with egg white. Bake above centre of oven for 20 to 25 minutes until pastry is golden brown.

MEN AND WOMEN AT WORK

Monday

Ham and coleslaw baps

Celery sticks

Fruit pie

Tuesday

☆ Sausage Vegetable Pie

Green salad

Raspberry mousse

Wednesday

★ Cheddar Gorgeous Soup

Crispy French bread and butter

Pork pie

Fresh fruit

Thursday

☆ Paprika chicken leg

Wholemeal roll and butter

Orange

★ Chewy Granola Bars

★ see recipe opposite
☆ see daily notes

Friday

☆ Sausages and spicy dip

Cream cheese and pineapple filled finger rolls

☆ Mincemeat Apple Oaties

Cheddar Gorgeous Soup

Monday

If you've no ham, use other cold cooked meat and mix with bought or home-made cole-slaw. Use homemade or bought fruit pie. **Pack:** fork. **For tomorrow:** make Sausage Vegetable Pie, see page 29. Prepare green salad. Make or buy raspberry mousse.

Tuesday

Take a separate, well-sealed container with salad dressing or mayonnaise. **Pack:** knife, fork and spoon. **For tomorrow:** make Cheddar Gorgeous Soup. Make or buy pork pie.

Wednesday

Pour heated soup into a vacuum flask. **Pack:** knife. **For tomorrow:** cook chicken leg. Peel and segment orange and pack in a small container. Make Chewy Granola Bars.

Thursday

Sprinkle cooked chicken leg with paprika. Spread whole-meal roll with butter and sand-wich together. **Pack:** nothing, fingers-only menu if you've peeled the orange. **For tomorrow:** grill sausages. Buy cream cheese and pineapple. Make Mincemeat Apple Oaties, see page 29.

Friday

Pack a favourite relish or pickle in a separate container as a dip. Wrap sausages in cling film or foil. Fill finger rolls with cream cheese. **Pack:** fork.

Cheddar Gorgeous Soup

A nourishing soup for chilly days. Pack in a vacuum flask.

For 4 portions

2 oz (50 g) butter
1 large onion, peeled and grated
1 large carrot, peeled and grated
1 oz (25 g) flour
½ level teaspoon dry mustard
1 pint (20 fl oz) chicken stock
½ level teaspoon paprika
¼ pint (5 fl oz) milk
¼ pint (5 fl oz) pale ale
8 oz (225 g) strong Cheddar cheese, grated
2 level tablespoons chopped parsley

1. Melt the butter in a sauce-pan. Add vegetables, cover and cook gently until soft but not browned; about 5 minutes.
2. Stir in flour and cook one minute. Remove from heat, add mustard and stir in stock gradually. Add paprika; return to heat and bring to the boil, stirring with a wooden spoon until thickened and smooth. Cover; simmer 15 to 20 mi-nutes, or until vegetables are tender.
3. Place soup in liquidiser goblet and run machine until mix-ture is smooth, or press through a sieve. Return the soup to a saucepan, stir in milk, ale and grated cheese. Heat gently, stirring, until cheese is melted and soup is warmed. Do not boil. Stir in parsley.

Chewy Granola Bars

Nuts and whole-grain cereals are available from most health food shops. Barley or rye flakes can be used instead of oats. Store bars in an airtight tin.

Makes 12 biscuits

1 oz (25 g) flaked almonds
1 oz (25 g) shelled hazelnuts
4 tablespoons vegetable oil
3 level tablespoons honey
2 oz (50 g) moist light brown sugar
4 oz (100 g) oat flakes
1 oz (25 g) desiccated coconut
1 oz (25 g) sesame seeds

1. Prepare a moderate oven (350°F, 180°C, Gas Mark 4). Grease a 7 in by 11 in shallow oblong tin.
2. Finely chop the almonds and hazelnuts. Measure the oil and honey into a bowl. Add the sugar and mix well.
3. Add the oat flakes, coconut, sesame seeds and nuts to the bowl and mix well. Press mix-ture into prepared tin. Bake in centre of oven for 25 minutes until golden.
4. Cool for 5 minutes in the tin, then mark into three along length and four across. Leave in the tin until warm, then remove carefully with a palette knife.

SCHOOL CHILDREN

Monday

☆ Cheesy carrot roll-ups

Crisps

Blackcurrant yogurt

Tuesday

☆ Sausage and cheese surprise

Buttered cheese crackers

★ Fruit Whip Flan

Wednesday

Ham flan

Coleslaw

☆ Orange jelly cups

Sponge fingers

Thursday

★ Tasty Turkey Spread rolls

Mandarin and banana salad

Peanuts

★ see recipe opposite
☆ see daily notes

Friday

☆ Fishy double deckers

Pea, carrot and sweetcorn salad

Lemon mousse

Tasty Turkey Spread

Monday

Add grated raw carrot to grated or cream cheese to make roll-ups, see page 43. **Pack:** spoon. **For tomorrow:** grill sausages. Make Fruit Whip Flan.

Tuesday

Cut cooked sausages into slices, cut cheese into cubes, put both in a container. **Pack:** fork and spoon. **For tomorrow:** buy or make ham flan and coleslaw. Cut two oranges in half, remove the flesh, make a pint of orange milk jelly, stir in the chopped segments, pour into orange shells to set.

Wednesday

Take orange milk cup(s) wrapped in cling film in a plastic container. **Pack:** fork and spoon. **For tomorrow:** make Tasty Turkey Spread. Peel and segment mandarin oranges (or satsumas, clementines, whatever is available) and put in a plastic container.

Thursday

Fill rolls. Slice a banana and sprinkle with lemon juice to prevent it going brown: add to oranges. **Pack:** spoon. **For tomorrow:** cook mixed veg for the salad. Make or buy a lemon mousse.

Friday

Make double decker sandwiches with fish paste or pâté, see page 41. Add salad cream and seasoning to mixed veg salad. **Pack:** fork and spoon.

Fruit Whip Flan

You can use different-flavoured jellies for this quick and easy flan which has a biscuit-crumb base. The lattice pattern on top is cleverly made with cocoa. Use the remainder for family supper.

For 6 portions

Crumb crust:
7.05 oz (200 g) packet digestive biscuits
4 oz (100 g) margarine

Filling:
1 fruit-flavoured jelly
½ pint (10 fl oz) boiling water
1 small can evaporated milk
Cocoa

1. Place biscuits between 2 sheets of greaseproof paper; crush finely with a rolling pin. Melt margarine in a saucepan, remove from heat and stir in the crumbs.
2. Turn the biscuit mixture into an 8½ in pie plate, press mixture on to the base and sides using a metal spoon. Chill until firm.
3. Place jelly in a basin; add boiling water and stir until dissolved, leave to cool, then place in the fridge until it is partially set.
4. Place evaporated milk in a bowl and whisk until thick. Gradually whisk in partially-set jelly. Pour mixture into the biscuit case.
5. Place some cocoa on a piece of greaseproof paper; coat a skewer in cocoa, then press lightly on to surface of dessert diagonally; repeat to make eight lines in all. Repeat lines in the other direction to form a lattice pattern. Keep in a cool place, such as the fridge, until ready to serve.

Tasty Turkey Spread

This spread is extra good left to mature in the fridge for two days before serving.

For 4 portions

1 set turkey giblets
1 turkey wing
1 medium-sized onion
2 cloves
1 bay leaf
Salt and pepper
4 rashers streaky bacon
2 oz (50 g) full fat soft cream cheese

1. Separate liver from giblets and reserve. Place remaining turkey giblets and wing in a medium-sized saucepan. Peel the onion, stick cloves into it and add to the pan with a bay leaf, 1 level teaspoon salt, a shake of pepper and 1 pint (20 fl oz) water.
2. Bring to boil, cover and simmer for about 1 hour. Add reserved liver for last 10 minutes of cooking time. Remove from heat and allow to cool. Place giblets and turkey on a board; cut meat off the wing, neck bones and gizzard. Discard bay leaf and cloves from onion. Finely mince or chop meats and cooked onion.
3. Remove rind and bone from the bacon, cut bacon into small pieces and fry over a low heat for 5 minutes.
4. Place minced turkey meat, onion and bacon mixture into a bowl. Add bacon fat from pan, 1 level teaspoon salt, a shake of pepper and cream cheese. Mix together until well blended.
5. Press turkey spread into a small serving bowl, cover and store in the fridge.

SCHOOL CHILDREN

Monday

☆ Nutty butter and banana sandwiches

Fruit stew

Sponge fingers

Tuesday

★ Cheese and Onion Roll

Baked beans

Apricot yogurt

Wednesday

☆ Sausage and cheese kebabs

Coleslaw

Cheese straws

Chocolate bar

Thursday

☆ Cold meat collation

☆ Three Cs salad

★ Rhubarb Ripple

★ *see recipe opposite*
☆ *see daily notes*

Friday

☆ Golden Chicken Bites

☆ Oaten Biscuits and butter

Orange salad

Mini Swiss roll

Rhubarb Ripple

Monday

Add mashed banana(s) to peanut butter for the sandwich filling. Stew one particular, or several kinds of fruit for the 'stew'. **Pack:** spoon. **For tomorrow:** make Cheese and Onion Roll.

Tuesday

Cut slices of Cheese and Onion Roll and wrap in cling film. Pack baked beans in a small individual container. **Pack:** knife, fork and spoon. **For tomorrow:** grill sausages for the kebabs. Make or buy coleslaw.

Wednesday

Spear short lengths of cubed sausages and chunks of hard cheese on to toothpicks for the kebabs. **Pack:** fork. **For tomorrow:** buy a selection of cold meats, eg luncheon meat, ham, liver sausage. Prepare grated raw carrot, celery and cress for the Three Cs salad. Make Rhubarb Ripple.

Thursday

Assemble the cold meat collation and Three Cs salad in separate containers. **Pack:** knife, fork and spoon. **For tomorrow:** make Golden Chicken Bites, see page 35. Make Oaten Biscuits, see page 17. Prepare orange salad, see under Wednesday, page 15.

Friday

Pack Oaten Biscuits in an airtight container. Pack butter separately. **Pack:** knife, spoon.

Cheese and Onion Roll

A nourishing dish, perfect for packed meals. Use leftovers warmed up for supper.

For 8 portions

1 medium-sized onion
8 oz (225 g) mature Cheddar cheese
4 slices bread from a large white loaf
6 tablespoons tomato ketchup
2 level teaspoons curry powder
1 level teaspoon salt
½ level teaspoon pepper
6 tablespoons milk
1 large (14 oz, 397 g) packet frozen puff pastry, just thawed
Milk or egg to glaze

1. Prepare a hot oven (425°F, 220°C, Gas Mark 7). Wet a 12in long baking sheet.
2. Peel the onion, chop finely and place in a bowl. Finely chop the cheese and add to bowl. Cut bread into ¼ in cubes and add to bowl with tomato ketchup, curry powder, salt, pepper, milk. Mix well.
3. Roll out the pastry and trim to an oblong 12 in by 10 in. Place cheese mixture in a line down half of the pastry, leaving a 1 in margin round the edge.
4. Brush the edges of pastry with milk or egg, fold pastry over filling and press edges together. Carefully lift roll on to prepared baking sheet. Holding knife parallel to the table, mark round edge of pastry to form flakes. Place finger firmly on pastry edge and cut into pastry at regular intervals to form flutes.
5. Make seven cuts diagonally across the top of the pastry; brush pastry with milk or egg.
6. Bake in centre of oven for 40 to 45 minutes until golden brown. Allow to cool slightly, then slide carefully on to a board or serving dish.

Rhubarb Ripple

This is a way of glamorising rhubarb to make it look like an exotic soft fruit. Pack into individual plastic containers.

For 4 portions

1 lb (½ kg) rhubarb
2 rounded tablespoons sugar
1 raspberry-flavoured jelly
1 small can evaporated milk

1. Trim the rhubarb, wipe stalks, then cut into 1 in lengths. Place in a saucepan with the sugar, cover with a lid and cook over a low heat until rhubarb is tender.
2. Pour into a liquidiser goblet, break up the jelly tablet and add, then run machine until mixture is smooth (alternatively, press rhubarb through a sieve into a saucepan, add jelly and stir over a low heat until jelly has dissolved). Pour into a bowl, cool, then place in the fridge until partially set. Pour evaporated milk into a bowl and place in the fridge to chill.
3. Whisk the evaporated milk until thick, then gradually whisk in all but 2 tablespoons of the rhubarb mixture. Pour into a bowl, then pour in the remaining rhubarb; gently cut through mixture with a spoon to swirl. Chill until firm.

SCHOOL CHILDREN

Monday

Meaty mayonnaise and celery baps

Cherry yogurt

Chocolate-covered sultanas

Tuesday

★ Continental Flan

Wholemeal roll and butter

☆ Orange jelly cups

Wednesday

☆ Frankfurter and pineapple kebabs

Crispy French bread and butter

★ Nut Crunch Cookies

Thursday

Crunchy chicken drumsticks

Cheese-filled celery sticks

Wholemeal roll and butter

☆ Apricot and Almond Tricorns

★ see recipe opposite
☆ see daily notes

Friday

Brown sardine roll-ups

Peanuts

Stewed fruit

Sponge fingers

Continental Flan

Monday

Use chopped cooked meat (or meat paste) mixed with chopped celery for the baps. **Pack:** spoon. **For tomorrow:** make Continental Flan. Make orange jelly cups, see under Tuesday, page 23.

Tuesday

Butter the halved wholemeal roll and sandwich together. **Pack:** knife, fork and spoon. **For tomorrow:** make Nut Crunch Cookies.

Wednesday

Spear frankfurter slices and cubes of canned pineapple on toothpicks for the kebabs. Cut a 5 in or 6 in piece of French bread, cut in half and butter then sandwich together again, for easy eating. **Pack:** nothing – a fingers-only menu. **For tomorrow:** coat chicken drumsticks in brown wholemeal flour before frying, for 'crunch'. Make Apricot and Almond Tricorns, see page 19.

Thursday

Fill celery sticks with cream cheese or grated hard cheese. **Pack:** fork. **For tomorrow:** drain a can of sardines and flake the fish. See page 43 for how to make roll-ups, use brown bread. Stew fruit.

Friday

Make sure the stewed fruit is sweet enough. The sponge fingers are fun to dip in it. **Pack:** spoon.

Continental Flan

Try this 'bread and butter' based flan. It is much quicker to prepare than the traditional shortcrust flans. Reserve a portion when serving for family supper or pack individual slices in foil and store in the freezer.

For 4 to 6 portions

Bread case:
1 oz (25 g) butter
8 or 9 slices bread from a large loaf

Filling:
2 eggs
1 bunch spring onions
3 oz (75 g) cheese
¼ pint (5 fl oz) milk
Salt and pepper
2 tomatoes
7 or 8 slices salami

1. Prepare a moderately hot oven (400°F, 200°C, Gas Mark 6).
2. Brush a little butter over the inside of an 8½ in ovenproof pie dish. Remove crusts from the bread and spread the bread with remaining butter. Line the dish with overlapping slices.
3. Bake on second shelf from top of oven for 15 minutes. Remove and reduce heat to 350°F, 180°C, Gas Mark 4.
4. Beat the eggs in a basin. Trim roots and tops from the spring onions; chop onions finely and add to eggs. Grate the cheese and mix into eggs with milk, salt and pepper.
5. Pour mixture into the bread case and bake on centre shelf for 25 minutes, until set.
6. Slice tomatoes and remove rind from salami slices. Arrange slices of tomato alternately with folded salami slices, around edge of flan. Return to oven for 5 minutes.

Nut Crunch Cookies

Packets of nut topping are available in most supermarkets. They give a lovely flavour and are cheaper than buying nuts. Store in an airtight tin.

Makes 30 biscuits

4 oz (100 g) margarine
4 oz (100 g) castor sugar
3 level tablespoons golden syrup
2 level tablespoons black treacle
1 egg
6 oz (150 g) wholewheat flour
1 oz (25 g) currants
3 oz (75 g) crunch-nut topping or chopped mixed nuts

1. Prepare a moderately hot oven (400°F, 200°C, Gas Mark 6). Grease a baking sheet.
2. Cut the margarine into small pieces and place in a bowl with the sugar. Measure syrup and treacle into bowl. Mix together, then beat for about 3 minutes until light and fluffy (or 2 minutes if using an electric mixer).
3. Beat the egg and add to the bowl gradually, beating well after each addition. Add flour, currants and 2 oz (50 g) crunch-nut topping. Mix well with a metal spoon.
4. Form the mixture into small balls with wetted hands. Spread remaining 1 oz (25 g) of crunch-nut topping on a plate. Press balls into topping, flattening them slightly. Invert on to baking sheets, placing biscuits well apart to allow for spreading. Bake just above centre of oven for 10 to 15 minutes until risen but still soft.
5. Cool biscuits 2 minutes, then remove with a palette knife and cool on a wire rack.

SCHOOL CHILDREN

Monday

Nutty cheese roll-ups

Orange salad

Fruit cake

Peanuts

Tuesday

★ Sausage Vegetable Pie

Carrot and pea salad

Fruit sponge flan

Wednesday

Egg and liver pâté rolls

Blackcurrant yogurt

☆ Chewy Granola Bars

Thursday

Ham and egg flan

Crunchy French bread and butter

Fruit trifle

Friday

☆ Tuna and carrot double deckers

Chunks of cheese

Crisps

★ Mincemeat Apple Oaties

★ see recipe opposite
☆ see daily notes

Mincemeat Apple Oaties

Monday

Mix peanut butter with grated cheese. To make roll-ups, see page 43. Peel and segment orange, satsuma, clementines, whatever you have. Sprinkle with castor sugar and put in a container. **Pack:** spoon. **For tomorrow:** make Sausage Vegetable Pie. Cook carrots and peas for salad. Make or buy fruit sponge flan.

Tuesday

Mix salad cream and a little seasoning with the cooked veg. **Pack:** knife, fork and spoon. **For tomorrow:** hard boil an egg. Make Chewy Granola Bars, see page 21.

Wednesday

Chop the hard-boiled egg and mix with a little salad cream. Use with liver pâté (or liver sausage) for the rolls. Pack: spoon. **For tomorrow:** make or buy ham and egg flan. Make or buy fruit trifle.

Thursday

Cut a piece of a large ham and egg flan, or one individual one, and wrap in cling film. Butter the French bread. **Pack:** fork and spoon. **For tomorrow:** drain and flake canned tuna fish and mix with grated raw carrot. Make Mincemeat Apple Oaties.

Friday

See page 41 for how to make double decker sandwiches. **Pack:** fork.

Sausage Vegetable Pie

This pie is also very good served hot for supper.

For 6 to 8 portions

Pastry:
10 oz (250 g) plain flour
½ level teaspoon salt
2½ oz (62.5 g) margarine
2½oz (62.5 g) lard

Filling:
1 lb (400 g) pork sausagemeat
1 large (15½ oz, 440 g) can mixed vegetable salad in mayonnaise
Beaten egg or milk to glaze

1. Prepare a moderate oven (400°F, 200°C, Gas Mark 6).
2. Place the flour and salt in a bowl. Add fats, cut into small pieces, and rub in until mixture resembles fine breadcrumbs. Add about 2½ tablespoons water and mix with a fork to form a firm dough. Turn out on to a floured board and knead lightly. Roll out two-thirds of the pastry and line an 8½ in oven-glass pie plate.
3. Press out half the sausagemeat, to cover the pastry in the dish. Spread contents of the can of vegetable salad over sausagemeat. Roll out remaining sausagemeat on a floured board to a circle, the same size as dish; place over vegetable salad.
4. Roll out the remaining pastry to cover pie. Brush rim of pastry with water; place over filling. Press edges together firmly; using the back of knife, cut edges of pastry to form flakes; flute edge.
5. Make a small hole in centre of pie. Brush pie with beaten egg or milk. Roll out pastry trimmings; cut out 'leaves'. Arrange around hole in pie; brush with egg or milk.
6. Place the pie on a baking sheet; bake in centre of oven for 1 hour, until golden brown.

Mincemeat Apple Oaties

A crunchy, nourishing 'sweet'.

Makes 20 bars

Shortcrust pastry made with 6 oz (175 g) plain flour
1 lb (½ kg) cooking apples
4 rounded tablespoons mincemeat

Topping:
4 oz (100 g) self-raising flour
4 oz (100 g) rolled (porridge) oats
2 oz (50 g) castor sugar
4 oz (100 g) margarine
2 level tablespoons golden syrup
Icing sugar

1. Prepare a moderate oven (375°F, 190°C, Gas Mark 5).
2. Roll out the pastry and line an 11 in by 7 in Swiss roll tin. Prick base and chill.
3. Peel and coarsely grate the cooking apples into a bowl, mix in the mincemeat. Spread in the pastry case.
4. Place the flour, oats, sugar in a bowl, add margarine, cut into small pieces and rub in.
5. Measure the golden syrup carefully and add to oat mixture and mix together with a fork to form a soft dough.
6. Turn out on to a floured board and knead lightly. Roll out to an oblong 11 in by 7 in, place oat topping over the mincemeat filling, press edges to seal. Prick all over top.
7. Bake in centre of oven for 35 to 40 minutes, until golden. Leave to cool in tin, cut into 20 bars. Dredge with icing sugar.

SLIMMERS

Monday

★ Pilchard and Cucumber Cocktail

Natural yogurt

Crispbread

Tuesday

☆ Chicken with raw mushrooms

Tomato, green pepper and onion salad

Fruit salad

Wednesday

☆ Cottage cheese with pimento

Stewed apples

Thursday

Low-calorie soup

Egg salad

★ Lemon Chiffon Cheesecake

★ see recipe opposite
☆ see daily notes

Friday

Cold lean lamb chop

Spring vegetable salad

Cottage cheese with chives

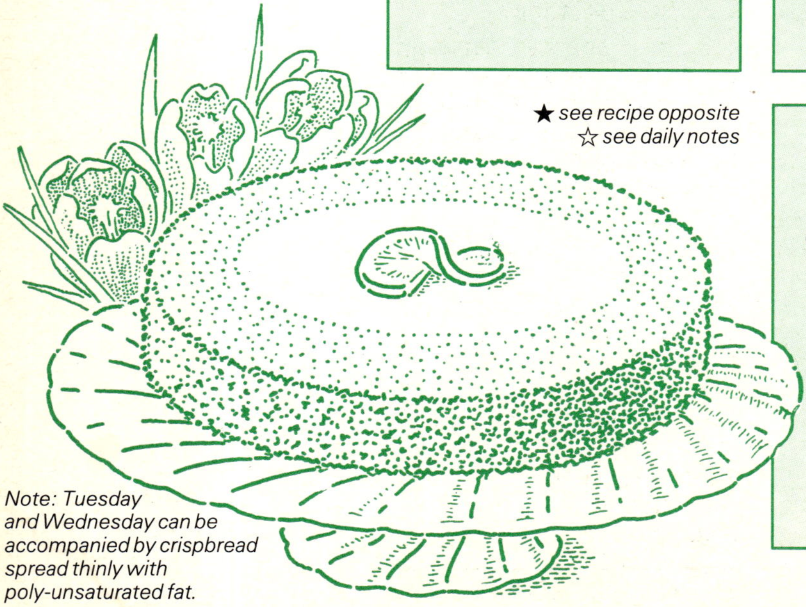

Note: Tuesday and Wednesday can be accompanied by crispbread spread thinly with poly-unsaturated fat.

Lemon Chiffon Cheesecake

Monday

Use chicken leftovers from the weekend, or cook a piece of chicken when you have the oven on. Chop the chicken and mix with the washed, sliced raw mushrooms. Prepare tomatoes, pepper and onion and put together in one container. Take low-calorie dressing in a separate container. **Pack:** knife, fork and spoon. **For tomorrow:** prepare Pilchard and Cucumber Cocktail.

Tuesday

Pack: fork and spoon, crispbread. **For tomorrow:** mix a carton of cottage cheese with chopped pimento. Stew the apples.

Wednesday

Pack: fork and spoon, crispbread. **For tomorrow:** buy or make low-calorie soup. Hard boil two eggs. Make Lemon Chiffon Cheesecake.

Thursday

Heat the low-calorie soup and take in a vacuum flask. Slice the eggs and take some low-calorie dressing in a separate container. **Pack:** forks. **For tomorrow:** cook a lean lamb chop. Cook, or save from supper, mixed spring vegetables. Buy a carton of cottage cheese and chives.

Friday

Chop and mix together the veg. Take a separate dressing. **Pack:** knife, fork and spoon, salt and pepper.

Pilchard and Cucumber Cocktail

Pack this in separate containers, cover and store in the fridge.

For 2 portions

1 small (5½ oz, 156 g) can pilchards
2 spring onions
4 oz (100 g) cottage cheese
Seasoning
1 level tablespoon low-calorie salad dressing
Sliced cucumber

1. Pour the liquor from can of pilchards into a small bowl. Halve the pilchards lengthwise; remove bones and discard. Roughly chop pilchards and place in a bowl.
2. Trim and wash the onions; roughly chop and add to the bowl with cheese and seasoning to taste. Lightly mix with a fork. Fold in salad dressing.

Lemon Chiffon Cheesecake

Cut this special slimmers' cheesecake into six portions, wrap in foil and freeze. Take out portions as you need them.

For 6 portions

4 starch-reduced digestive biscuits
1 level teaspoon ground cinnamon
1 medium-sized lemon
½ oz (1 envelope, gelatine
1 large (8 oz, 227 g) carton cottage cheese
1 (5.3 oz, 150 g) carton natural low-fat yogurt
1 scant teaspoon liquid sweetener
2 egg whites

1. Place the biscuits in a polythene bag; crush finely with a rolling pin. Add cinnamon and shake to mix. Brush a round 6 in loose-bottomed cake tin with melted oil. Place biscuit crumbs in tin and toss until the tin is coated. Remove excess crumbs and reserve.
2. Grate lemon rind; reserve. Squeeze juice and place in a measuring jug; make up to ¼ pint (5 fl oz) with water. Add gelatine and stir. Place jug in a pan of water over a moderate heat and stir until all the gelatine has dissolved.
3. Sieve the cottage cheese into a bowl. Add yogurt gradually, beating well until smooth. Beat dissolved gelatine, lemon rind and liquid sweetener into cottage cheese mixture. Place in fridge until it is on the point of setting.
4. Whisk the egg whites until stiff, but not dry; fold into the cheese mixture. Pour into tin; return to fridge until set.

SLIMMERS

Monday

Grapefruit segments

☆ Stuffed tomatoes

Edam cheese slices

Tuesday

☆ White fish with celery and apple salad

Banana

Wednesday

★ Chicken and Savoury Rice

Lemon mousse

Thursday

Cold roast lamb slices

★ Picuto Salad

☆ Pineapple rice

Note: Tuesday and Friday can be accompanied by crispbread spread thinly with poly-unsaturated fat.

★ *see recipes opposite*
☆ *see daily notes*

Friday

Spring vegetable soup

★ Shrimpers Boats

Stewed pears

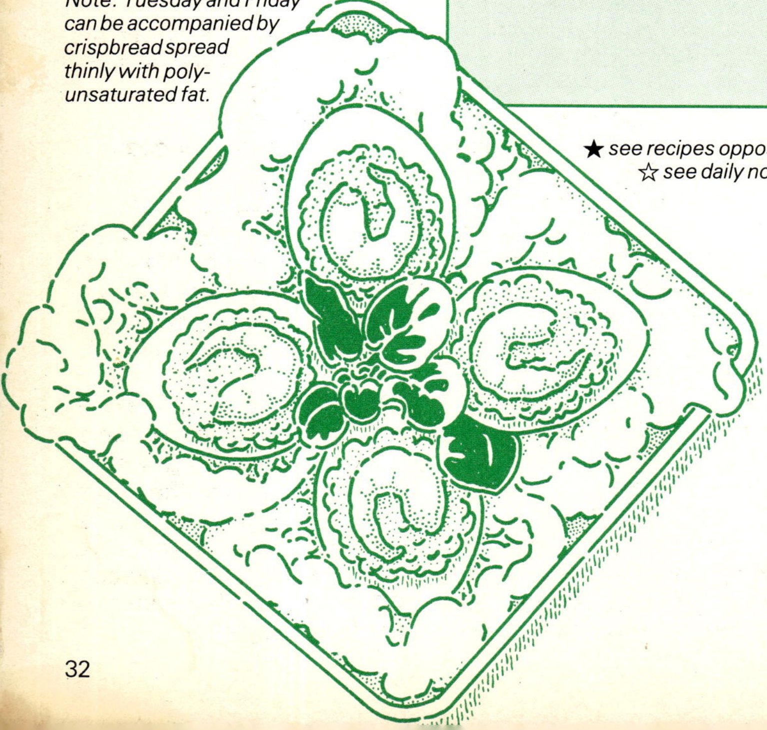

Shrimpers Boats

Monday

Use a third or half a can of unsweetened grapefruit segments, or prepare fresh fruit the night before. Stuff tomatoes with leftover pieces of ham and mushroom and cook over the weekend when you have the oven on. **Pack:** spoon and fork. **For tomorrow:** cook white fish for salad and flake when cold.

Tuesday

Cut up apple and celery and mix together with a little lemon juice, add fish. **Pack:** fork, crispbread. **For tomorrow:** make Chicken and Savoury Rice. Make or buy lemon mousse.

Wednesday

Place the heated Chicken and Savoury Rice in a wide-necked vacuum flask. **Pack:** fork and spoon. **For tomorrow:** have ready some cold meat. Make Picuto Salad. Cook ground rice. Buy fresh pineapple.

Thursday

Put cold meat slices on a paper plate and wrap in cling film. Place a slice or two of fresh pineapple on top of the ground rice. **Pack:** knife, fork and spoon. **For tomorrow:** buy or make low-calorie spring vegetable soup. Make Shrimpers Boats. Stew pears.

Friday

Pour the heated soup into a vacuum flask. **Pack:** fork and spoon, crispbread.

Chicken and Savoury Rice

Keep the spare portion covered in the fridge for a few days, or in the freezer for a month. Take to work in a wide-necked vacuum flask.

For 2 portions

2 small chicken portions
1 stick celery
Salt and pepper
½ teaspoon oregano
1 bay leaf
1 tomato
2 oz (50 g) long-grain rice
4 oz (100 g) frozen peas
4 oz (100 g) frozen green beans

1. Wash the chicken portions and place them in a saucepan. Pour in enough water to cover.
2. Wash and slice the celery, add to the saucepan with salt and pepper, oregano and bay leaf. Bring to boil, cover and simmer for 35 to 40 minutes.
3. Remove the chicken and bay leaf from the stock, allow to cool slightly and remove chicken skin. Cut meat from the bone into pieces; reserve. Skin and chop the tomatoes.
4. Pour ¾ pint (15 fl oz) stock into a saucepan, bring to boil and add rice with peas and beans, season to taste. Bring back to boil and simmer for 15 to 20 minutes, stirring occasionally, adding extra stock if necessary until water is absorbed and rice is tender.
5. Remove from the heat, stir in chicken pieces, tomato and any celery left in the stock.

Picuto Salad

Pack individual portions of this salad on paper or plastic plates and cover with cling film. It will keep very well in the fridge for a few days.

For 3 portions

3 large tomatoes
6 pickled baby dill cucumbers
Lemon juice
Salt
Black pepper
Chopped parsley

1. Slice the tomatoes and pickled dill cucumbers. Arrange slices of tomato, overlapping, around the edge of a plate. Pile the sliced cucumber in the centre of the salad.
2. Sprinkle the tomato and cucumber with a little lemon juice, salt, black pepper and chopped parsley.

Shrimpers Boats

Place the filled 'boats' on a paper or plastic plate and cover with cling film.

For 2 portions

4 eggs
4 oz (100 g) fresh or defrosted shrimps
2 teaspoons anchovy essence
1 level tablespoon low-calorie salad dressing
Shake of pepper
1 teaspoon freshly chopped parsley

1. Hard boil the eggs for 10 minutes; crack the shells and leave to cool in cold water. Halve the eggs lengthwise and place the yolks in a small bowl; mash until smooth.
2. Peel the fresh shrimps if you're using them, and reserve a few for garnish; roughly chop the remainder. Add the chopped shrimps and remaining ingredients to the yolks; mix.
3. Divide the mixture between egg halves; garnish with the reserved shrimps.

MEN AND WOMEN AT WORK

Monday

☆ Meaty coleslaw rolls

Dutch apple pie

Tuesday

☆ Beano Flan

Tomato and new potato salad

Crusty French bread and butter

Flapjack

Wednesday

★ Golden Chicken Bites

Green salad

Wholemeal buttered roll

Fresh fruit salad

Thursday

☆ Cheesy carrot roll

Tomato and sweetcorn salad

★ Cherry Anzac Biscuits

Friday

☆ Sardine snack sandwiches

☆ Spicy Raisin Cheesecake

★ see recipe opposite
☆ see daily notes

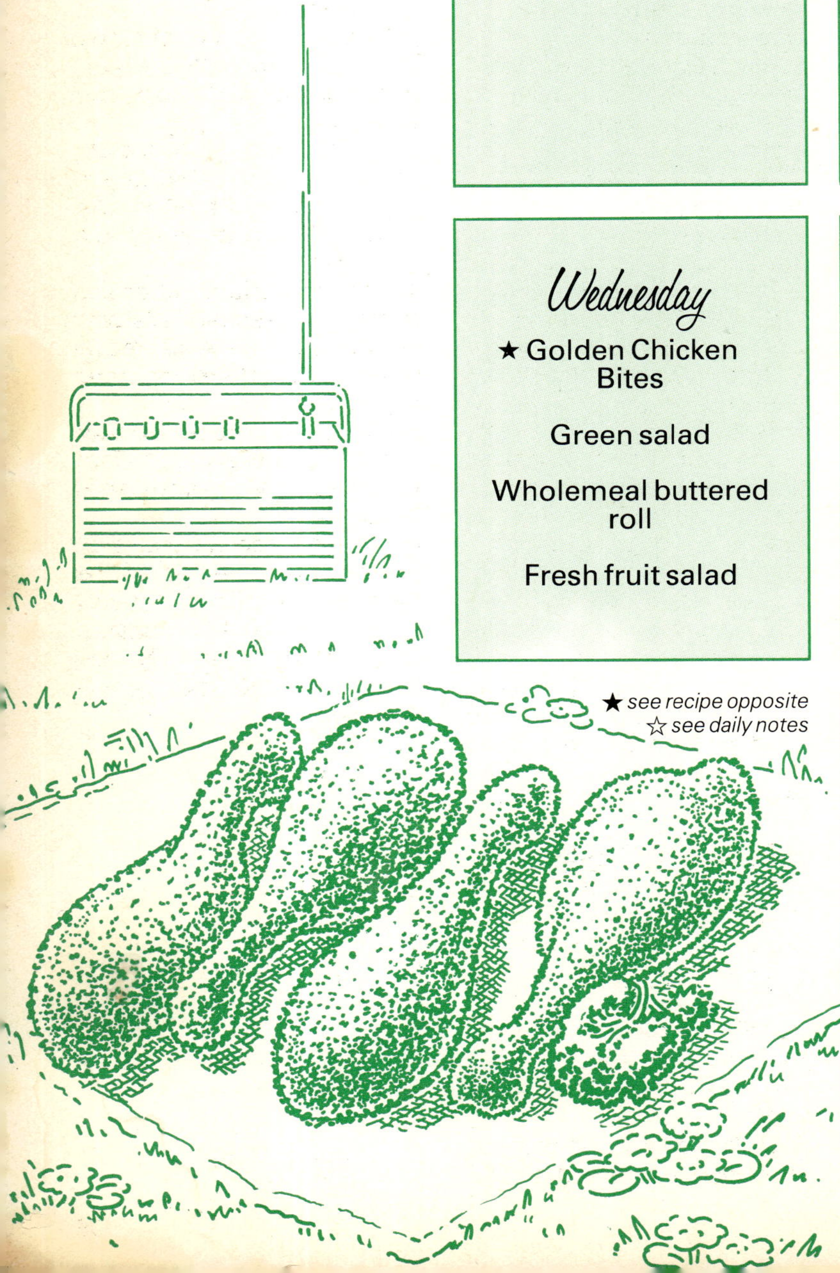

Golden Chicken Bites

Monday

Chop meat or poultry leftovers from Sunday and mix with shredded raw cabbage and grated raw carrot; moisten with coleslaw dressing. Dutch apple pie has sultanas and cinnamon mixed with the apple, if you didn't have it for Sunday pud, pack a portion of what you did have. **Pack:** spoon. **For tomorrow:** make Beano Flan, see page 43. Cook some potatoes. Buy or make flapjack.

Tuesday

Pack: knife and fork. **For tomorrow:** make Golden Chicken Bites. Prepare green salad. Prepare fruit for salad.

Wednesday

Pack: fork and spoon. **For tomorrow:** grate cheese and raw carrot. Make Cherry Anzac Biscuits.

Thursday

Mix grated cheese and grated raw carrot for the roll filling. Make tomato and sweetcorn salad. **Pack:** fork. **For tomorrow:** make Spicy Raisin Cheesecake, see page 43.

Friday

For sardine snack sandwiches, drain the sardines, mash then mix with slices of cucumber. **Pack:** spoon.

Golden Chicken Bites

The flavour of orange adds tang to these drumsticks. They travel well and can conveniently be made in advance.

Makes 6

Half an orange
1 oz (25 g) browned breadcrumbs
1 level teaspoon mixed dried herbs
Pinch ground ginger
1 egg
6 chicken drumsticks
Salt and pepper
1 oz (25 g) butter

1. Prepare a moderate oven (350°F, 180°C, Gas Mark 4).
2. Finely grate the orange rind and mix with breadcrumbs, herbs and ginger.
3. Beat the egg with 1 tablespoon water on a plate. Sprinkle chicken drumsticks with a little salt and pepper. Spread breadcrumbs on a sheet of greaseproof paper; dip chicken in egg, then coat in breadcrumbs, press them on firmly.
4. Melt the butter in a roasting tin, add chicken and baste with butter. Bake in the centre of oven for 30 to 35 minutes until deep golden brown.

Chewy Anzac Biscuits

These are both nourishing and delicious. You will have no trouble persuading the family to eat any not packed!

Makes about 25

2 oz (50 g) glacé cherries
4 oz (100 g) plain flour
4 oz (100 g) rolled (porridge) oats
3 oz (75 g) desiccated coconut
8 oz (200 g) castor sugar
1 level tablespoon golden syrup
4 oz (100 g) butter
1½ level teaspoons bicarbonate of soda
2 tablespoons boiling water

1. Grease two baking sheets. Prepare a cool oven (300°F, 150°C, Gas Mark 2).
2. Finely chop the cherries. Place in a bowl with the flour, oats, coconut and sugar; mix together well.
3. Measure the syrup carefully into a small pan. Add butter and heat gently until melted. Dissolve the bicarbonate of soda in boiling water.
4. Add the melted butter and syrup and dissolved bicarbonate of soda to the dry ingredients. Stir together to mix thoroughly.
5. Divide the mixture into balls about the size of a walnut. Place well apart on baking sheets and flatten slightly.
6. Bake on second and third shelves from the top of the oven for 20 to 25 minutes until golden brown. Cool slightly, then remove carefully and leave to cool completely on a wire rack.

MEN AND WOMEN AT WORK

Monday

Cold meat and salad rolls

Gooseberry crumble

Tuesday

☆ Sunny Salami Loaf

Tomato, egg and cucumber salad

★ Plum Cloud

Wednesday

Cheese and onion pasties

Coleslaw salad

Fresh fruit trifle

Thursday

Pork pie and pickle

Green salad

Wheatmeal roll and butter

☆ Strawberry Foam and sponge fingers

★ *see recipes opposite*
☆ *see daily notes*

Friday

★ Frankfurter Salad Kebabs

Crusty French bread and butter

☆ Scones and fresh raspberry mush

Frankfurter Salad Kebabs

Monday

Use leftover Sunday pud packed in a plastic container. **Pack:** spoon. **For tomorrow:** prepare Sunny Salami Loaf, see page 45. Hard-boil eggs and prepare salad. Make Plum Cloud.

Tuesday

Pack: fork and spoon. **For tomorrow:** make or buy cheese and onion pasties, coleslaw and fresh fruit trifle.

Wednesday

Pack: knife, fork and spoon. **For tomorrow:** buy pork pie. Prepare green salad. Make Strawberry Foam, see page 45.

Thursday

Pack the pickle in a small container. **Pack:** knife, fork and spoon. **For tomorrow:** prepare Frankfurter Salad Kebabs. Make or buy scones and make fresh raspberry mush by mashing up fresh raspberries with castor sugar.

Friday

Pack fresh raspberry mush separately in a small plastic container. Butter the scones and sandwich together. **Pack:** knife.

Plum Cloud

This fresh fruit mousse is a perfect refresher on a hot day. It freezes well when packed in individual plastic containers. Use gooseberries and blackcurrants this way when they are in season.

Makes 4 portions

1 lb (½ kg) plums
Castor sugar
Red food colouring
2 egg whites
¼ pint (5 fl oz) pint whipping cream

1. Remove stones from plums. Place in a medium-sized saucepan with 1 tablespoon of water. Cover with a lid and cook over a low heat for about 5 minutes until soft and pulpy.
2. Rub the fruit through a sieve into a large mixing bowl, stir in the sugar to taste, about 3 oz (75 g). Add a few drops of red food colouring to colour purée red. Cool completely.
3. Place the egg whites in a bowl, whisk until stiff but not dry. Whisk in 1 rounded tablespoon sugar. Reserve 2 tablespoons purée in a small bowl, gradually whisk egg whites into remainder.
4. Place the cream in a bowl. Whisk until it just holds its shape in soft peaks. Reserve 2 tablespoons, then fold remainder into fruit mixture, cutting through mixture with a metal spoon until combined.
5. Pour mixture into four individual containers chill. Just before serving place a spoonful of reserved cream on each sundae and drizzle over the reserved fruit purée. Serve for supper, reserving a portion or pack individually in the freezer.

Frankfurter Salad Kebabs

Place kebabs in a plastic container and cover with foil to keep in place before putting on the lid.

Makes 6 kebabs

6 oz (175 g) Edam cheese
6 small, firm tomatoes
1 medium-sized green pepper
3 in piece of cucumber
1 small (8 oz, 227 g) can cocktail frankfurters
12 small sprigs of watercress
12 small lettuce leaves

1. Cut the cheese into 18 small cubes. Cut tomatoes in halves. Cut the pepper in half lengthwise; discard seeds, core and white pith. Cut pepper into 18 pieces.
2. Cut the cucumber into 9 slices; cut each slice in half. Drain frankfurters.
3. On each of 6 skewers, arrange 3 cubes of cheese, 3 pieces of green pepper, 3 pieces of cucumber, 2 or 3 frankfurters, 2 tomato halves, 2 sprigs of watercress and 2 lettuce leaves.

MEN AND WOMEN AT WORK

Monday

Crunchy corned beef and tomato roll

☆ Creamy egg roll-ups

Gooseberry fool

Tuesday

Sausages and relish dip

★ Beans Toulouse

Wholemeal roll and butter

Fruit pie

Wednesday

★ Gala Cheese Salad

Crusty French bread and butter

Fruit trifle

Thursday

☆ Paprika drumsticks

New potato and pea salad

★ Chocolate Nut Bars

★ see recipe opposite
☆ see daily notes

Friday

Creamy fish vol-au-vents

Tomato and spring onion salad

Fresh fruit flan

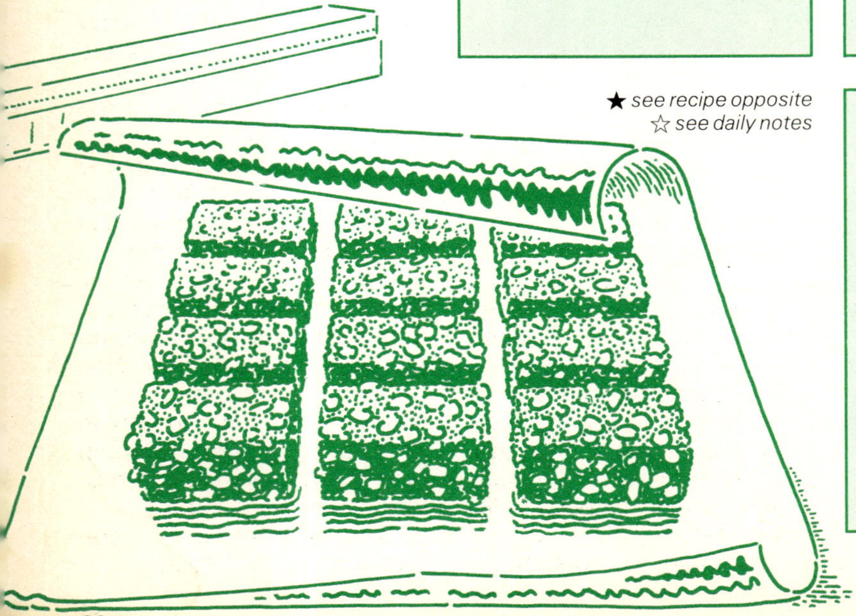

Chocolate Nut Bars

Monday

Creamy egg roll-ups: chop hard boiled eggs, season and add mayonnaise, then see page 43. Use leftover Sunday pud or fresh fruit. **Pack:** spoon. **For tomorrow:** grill sausages. Prepare Beans Toulouse. Make or buy fruit pie.

Tuesday

Cheer up cold cooked sausages with a small container of favourite relish. **Pack:** fork and spoon. **For tomorrow:** prepare Gala Cheese Salad. Make or buy fruit trifle.

Wednesday

Pack: knife, fork and spoon. **For tomorrow:** cook chicken drumsticks. Prepare new potato and pea salad. Cook Chocolate Nut Bars.

Thursday

Sprinkle drumsticks with paprika. Add mayonnaise to salad. **Pack:** knife and fork. **For tomorrow:** bake vol-au-vent cases and fill with a cooked fish and white sauce mixture. Make or buy fresh fruit flan.

Friday

Pack vol-au-vents separately in a plastic container. **Pack:** knife, fork and spoon.

Beans Toulouse

This delicious salad will keep for a day or two in the fridge.

For 4 to 6 portions

1 lb (1/2 kg) French beans
1 oz (25 g) butter
2 rounded tablespoons sliced spring onion
2 oz (50 g) garlic sausage
Paprika

1. Top, tail and wash the beans. Melt the butter in a saucepan, add onion and fry gently for about a minute. Add the beans, cover and cook gently for 10 to 15 minutes, shaking pan occasionally, until just tender.
2. Cut the garlic sausage into thin strips, add to the pan and stir until heated through. When cool pack into individual portions as required.

Gala Cheese Salad

Prepare individual portions and pack in plastic containers.

For 4 portions

1 pack (1/4 lb, 100 g) sliced ham sausage
1 stick of celery
1 in piece of cucumber
3/4 lb (350 g) cottage cheese with chives
1 level tablespoon salad cream
1/4 level teaspoon salt
Pepper
6 lettuce leaves
1 medium-sized tomato

1. Reserve 3 slices of the ham sausage for garnish. Roughly chop the remainder.
2. Wash and slice the celery. Cut cucumber into 1/2 in cubes. Place the chopped ham sausage, celery, cucumber, cottage cheese with chives, salad cream, salt and a shake of pepper in a bowl; mix together.
3. Wash the lettuce leaves and place in a serving bowl or divide into individual containers. Pile cottage cheese mixture in centre of lettuce.
4. Cut reserved slices of ham sausage into halves. Fold each halved slice around to make a cone and place around edge of cottage cheese. Cut the tomato into 6 wedges; place a wedge inside each cone.

Chocolate Nut Bars

Wrap in foil or cling film to transport. Store in a tin in the fridge for up to 5 days; or in the freezer for up to 3 months.

Makes 12

3 oz (75 g) semi-sweet biscuits
4 level tablespoons golden syrup
4 level tablespoons cocoa
4 oz (100 g) icing sugar
4 oz (100 g) margarine
3 oz (75 g) salted peanuts

1. Lightly grease a shallow, 7 in square cake tin. Place the biscuits between two sheets of greaseproof paper; crush finely with a rolling pin. Measure syrup carefully. Place in a saucepan with cocoa, icing sugar and margarine.
2. Place saucepan over a gentle heat until margarine has melted. Remove from heat and stir in crushed biscuits and 2 oz (50 g) peanuts until evenly coated in chocolate mixture. Turn out mixture into a tin and spread evenly. Coarsely chop the remaining peanuts and sprinkle over the top of the chocolate mixture; level top with back of metal spoon pressing peanuts down lightly.
3. Cool, then place in fridge until set; cut into 12 bars.

MEN AND WOMEN AT WORK

Monday

☆ Spicy meat and salad double deckers

☆ Chivey potato salad

Blackcurrant pie

Tuesday

☆ Danish stuffed eggs

★ Courgette Raita

Wholemeal rolls and butter

Fruit jelly

Wednesday

Cheese and onion flan

Watercress and tomato salad

Raspberry mousse

Thursday

☆ Wholemeal chicken pasties

★ Curried French Beans

☆ Apricot Flan

Friday

★ Kipper Loaf

Crusty French bread and butter

Fresh fruit salad

★ see recipe opposite
☆ see daily notes

Curried French Bean Salad

Monday

Spicy meat and salad double deckers: fill two slices of bread with cold sliced meat sprinkled with paprika, fill two more slices with a salad mixture and mayonnaise; cut both sandwiches together into fingers. It looks attractive to use brown bread for one sandwich, white for the other. Chivey potato salad: slice cooked potatoes and mix with chopped chives and mayonnaise. Blackcurrant pie can be bought or use home-made leftovers from Sunday. **Pack:** fork and spoon. **For tomorrow:** hard boil eggs. Prepare courgettes and dressing. Make fruit jelly.

Tuesday

Halve the eggs lengthwise, mix yolks with Danish Blue cheese and repack in white halves. **Pack:** fork and spoon. **For tomorrow:** buy or make cheese and onion flan. Prepare salad. Make or buy mousse.

Wednesday

Pack: fork and spoon. **For tomorrow:** use wholemeal flour to make the pastry for the chicken pasties. Prepare Curried French Beans. Make Apricot Flan, see page 49.

Thursday

Pack: fork and spoon. **For tomorrow:** make Kipper Loaf. Prepare fresh fruit salad.

Friday

Pack: fork and spoon.

Courgette Raita

The fresh-tasting yogurt makes a quick dressing for this salad.

For 4 portions

8 oz (225 g) small courgettes
Salt
1 (5.3 oz, 150 g) carton natural yogurt
2 level teaspoons German or Meaux mustard
Paprika

1. Wash and trim the courgettes. Cut into thin slices and layer with salt in a colander or sieve; leave for 30 minutes to drain. Pat dry on kitchen paper.
2. Place yogurt and mustard in a bowl; mix well. Gently turn the courgettes in the mixture to coat. Sprinkle top with paprika.

Curried French Bean Salad

Mild and creamy curry sauce is really delicious when served with crunchy French beans.

For 4 portions

1 lb (½ kg) French beans
Knob of butter
Salt
2 rounded tablespoons thick mild mayonnaise
2 level teaspoons curry paste
2 level teaspoons tomato ketchup
1 teaspoon lemon juice
A few toasted flaked almonds

1. Top, tail and wash the beans. Place in a saucepan with 3 tablespoons water, butter and some salt. Bring to the boil, reduce heat, cover and cook gently for 10 to 15 minutes until beans are tender. Drain and cool quickly.
2. Mix mayonnaise, curry paste, ketchup and lemon juice in a basin.
3. Pour curry mayonnaise on to beans and sprinkle with flaked almonds.

Kipper Loaf

This will store in foil for up to 5 days in a fridge. Alternatively, wrap individual portions securely in foil, place in a freezer bag, label and store for up to 3 months in a freezer.

For 8 portions

2 (10 oz) packs frozen buttered kipper fillets
3 oz (75 g) butter
½ lemon
4 oz (100 g) fresh white breadcrumbs
¼ level teaspoon pepper
1 small (7¼ oz, 206 g) can vegetable salad
1 tomato
Lettuce

1. Line base and sides of a 1 lb (1½ pint capacity) loaf tin with foil overlapping the rim by 2 in at each side.
2. Cook the kippers as directed. Empty one pack into liquidiser goblet, add half the butter and run machine until contents are blended. Place in a bowl and repeat with remaining kippers and butter. Alternatively, place cooked kippers and butter in a bowl and mash with a fork.
3. Squeeze the juice from the lemon and add to the bowl. Mix in breadcrumbs and pepper.
4. Place half of the mixture in the tin; level with a spoon and press down. Cover with contents of can of vegetable salad. Spread with remaining kipper mixture. Press down level.
5. Bring the foil from each side of the tin to cover top; leave loaf in the fridge overnight.
6. Open foil and invert loaf on to a serving dish.

SCHOOL CHILDREN

Monday

☆ Meaty salad baps

Fruit trifle

Flapjack or shortbread

Banana

Tuesday

★ Beano Flan

Strawberry mousse

Cheese straws

Apple

Wednesday

Yeasty tomato sandwiches

☆ Golden Chicken Bites

Fruit yogurt

Chocolate bar

Thursday

☆ Fish and cress roll-ups

Cheese and onion pasty

Packet of nuts

Fresh fruit salad

★ see recipes opposite
☆ see daily notes

Friday

Ham and lettuce roll

Crisps

Tomato and carrot salad

★ Spicy Raisin Cheesecake

Spicy Raisin Cheesecake

Monday

Baps: use leftover Sunday joint or canned meat or paste. Use leftover pud and cake too, making up Vitamin C content if necessary with fresh fruit or lots of fresh fruit juice. **Pack:** spoon. **For tomorrow:** make Beano Flan. Buy or make strawberry mousse and cheese straws.

Tuesday

Pack: fork and spoon. **For tomorrow:** prepare Golden Chicken Bites, see page 35.

Wednesday

Spread sandwiches with butter and yeast extract and fill with sliced tomatoes. **Pack:** spoon. **For tomorrow:** make or buy cheese and onion pasty. Why not have fresh fruit salad for supper and store extra in the fridge.

Thursday

Fish and cress roll-ups: cut the crust off each slice of bread, then roll out flat with a rolling pin. Butter, then add flaked canned fish (or fish paste) and cress, then roll up tightly like a Swiss roll. **Pack:** spoon. **For tomorrow:** prepare grated raw carrots. Make Spicy Raisin Cheesecake.

Friday

Pack: fork and spoon.

Beano Flan

Serve for supper tonight and cling-wrap a piece for tomorrow. Or cut into portions and pack and freeze individually.

For 4 to 6 portions

1 small (7 oz, 198 g) packet frozen puff pastry, just thawed

Filling:

2 eggs

3 tablespoons milk

2 oz (50 g) Cheddar cheese

1 small (7¾ oz, 220 g) can baked beans with pork sausages

¼ level teaspoon salt

Pepper

1. Prepare a hot oven (425°F, 220°C, Gas Mark 7).
2. Make pastry as directed on the packet, roll out and line an 8 in flan tin. Prick all over the base: chill.
3. To prepare the filling: beat the eggs and milk together in a bowl. Grate the cheese and add to the bowl with the contents of the can of baked beans and sausages. Season with salt and pepper and mix well.
4. Pour into the pastry case and bake in the centre of the oven for 25 minutes.
5. Remove the flan ring and cook a further 5 to 10 minutes until the pastry is a golden brown.

Spicy Raisin Cheesecake

This cheesecake freezes well. Pack individual portions in foil and serve the remainder for family supper.

For 8 portions

Base:

½ lb (225 g) digestive biscuits

4 oz (100 g) butter

Filling:

2 eggs

4 oz (100 g) cottage cheese

1 (5 fl oz, 150 g) carton soured cream

1 rounded tablespoon castor sugar

4 oz (100 g) seedless raisins

1 level teaspoon mixed spice

½ teaspoon vanilla essence

1. Prepare a moderate oven (350°F, 180°C, Gas Mark 4).
2. Place the digestive biscuits between 2 sheets of greaseproof paper and crush finely with a rolling pin.
3. Melt the butter in a medium-sized saucepan; stir in crushed biscuits. Press the mixture on the base and around the sides of a 9 in loose-based flan tin.
4. Separate the eggs; place the yolks in a basin and whites in a clean, grease-free bowl. Press the cottage cheese through a nylon sieve into the basin. Add the soured cream, castor sugar, raisins, mixed spice and vanilla essence to the cottage cheese and egg yolks and mix well together.
5. Whisk the egg whites until stiff, but not dry. Fold into the cheese mixture. Place on the biscuit base, and cook in the centre of the oven for about 30 to 35 minutes, until the mixture has set.
6. Remove from the oven and leave to cool. When cold, carefully remove the flan tin.

SCHOOL CHILDREN

Monday

☆ Chopped cooked meat and salad

☆ Nutty cream cheese roll

Fruit yogurt

Tuesday

★ Sunny Salami Loaf

Fresh fruit salad

Sponge fingers

Peanuts

Wednesday

☆ Fruit and nut chicken salad

Wholemeal roll and butter

☆ Plum Cloud

Chocolate bar

Thursday

Tasty tuna fish rolls

Tomato and cucumber salad

★ Strawberry Foam

★ *see recipe opposite*
☆ *see daily notes*

Friday

☆ Frankfurter Salad Kebabs

Crusty French bread and butter

Blackcurrant pie

Chocolate raisins

Strawberry Foam

Monday

Mix chopped cooked meat (or canned luncheon meat) with tomatoes, cress, cucumber etc and mayonnaise. For the roll add chopped walnuts or chopped mixed nuts to the cream cheese. **Pack:** fork and spoon. **For tomorrow:** prepare Sunny Salami Loaf. Make fruit salad.

Tuesday

Pack: spoon. **For tomorrow:** prepare chicken salad by chopping cooked chicken and adding whatever you like such as grated carrot, tomatoes, cucumber and so on, plus chopped nuts and sultanas or chopped dates, moisten with salad cream or French dressing. Make Plum Cloud, see page 37.

Wednesday

Pack: fork and spoon. **For tomorrow:** prepare salad. Make Strawberry Foam.

Thursday

If liked, use a little salad cream to moisten the tuna fish. **Pack:** fork and spoon. **For tomorrow:** prepare Frankfurter Salad Kebabs, see page 37. Make or buy a blackcurrant pie.

Friday

Pack: fork.

Sunny Salami Loaf

Choose a bright pink inexpensive salami for this stuffed loaf. It will keep well in the fridge for a day. Wrap individual portions in foil or cling film.

Makes 8 to 10 slices

1 small crusty white loaf
4 spring onions
6 oz (175 g) salami
1 (7 oz, 198 g) can sweetcorn niblets
1 level teaspoon salt
Pepper
6 rounded tablespoons salad cream
Butter

1. Split loaf in half lengthwise. Pull out the soft bread, taking care not to break the crust; make into breadcrumbs and place in a bowl.
2. Trim and chop the spring onions. Remove rind, then chop salami. Drain contents of can of sweetcorn. Add sweetcorn to breadcrumbs with spring onions, salami, salt, pepper and salad cream; mix well.
3. Butter the inside of the loaf. Stuff loaf with filling mixture, press loaf firmly together, wrap in foil and leave in the fridge.

Strawberry Foam

Use up squashy over-ripe strawberries this way. It is quickly made in a liquidiser goblet. Pour into individual moulds or make in a large mould for a family meal.

For 4 to 6 portions

1 large orange
3 sugar cubes
12 oz (350 g) strawberries
2 envelopes (1 oz) gelatine
2 oz (50 g) castor sugar

1. Scrub the orange. Rub the skin all over with the sugar cubes until sugar has absorbed the zest. Cut a thin slice from centre of orange, reserve for decoration. Pare a slice of rind thinly from one half of the orange, reserve. Squeeze juice. Hull strawberries, reserving 5 for decoration.
2. Measure 4 tablespoons cold water into a small basin, add gelatine and stir. Place basin in a pan of water over a moderate heat; stir until gelatine has completely dissolved.
3. Place sugar cubes, orange juice, strawberries, gelatine and castor sugar in liquidiser goblet, run machine until mixture is well blended. Top up to 1 pint with cold water. Place liquidiser goblet in fridge to chill, until mixture is half set. (If liquidiser is not large enough, pour mixture into a bowl.)
4. Return liquidiser goblet to machine and run until pale and fluffy and almost doubled in volume. (Or whisk in a bowl.)
5. Pour mixture into a 1½ pint fluted jelly mould, or individual moulds. Chill until firm.
6. To unmould: dip jelly mould into hot water for a few seconds, invert on to a serving plate.
7. Shred reserved orange rind finely with a sharp knife. Cut reserved orange slice into quarters. Slice four reserved strawberries into three. Arrange strawberry slices and shredded peel around serving plate. Place two orange wedges and a whole strawberry on top of jelly.

SCHOOL CHILDREN

Monday

☆ Moist meat sandwiches

Fruit yogurt

Mini Swiss roll

Crisps

Tuesday

Crispy bacon and tomato roll

☆ Egg and cress roll-ups

★ Gooseberry Flapjack Tart

Wednesday

☆ Gala Cheese Salad

Crusty French bread and butter

Orange mousse and sponge fingers

Thursday

☆ Ham and veg double deckers

Mini sausages

☆ Chocolate Nut Bars

★ *see recipe opposite*
☆ *see daily notes*

Friday

★ Crispy Mackerel Salad

Finger rolls and butter

Peanuts

Fresh strawberries, plums or cherries

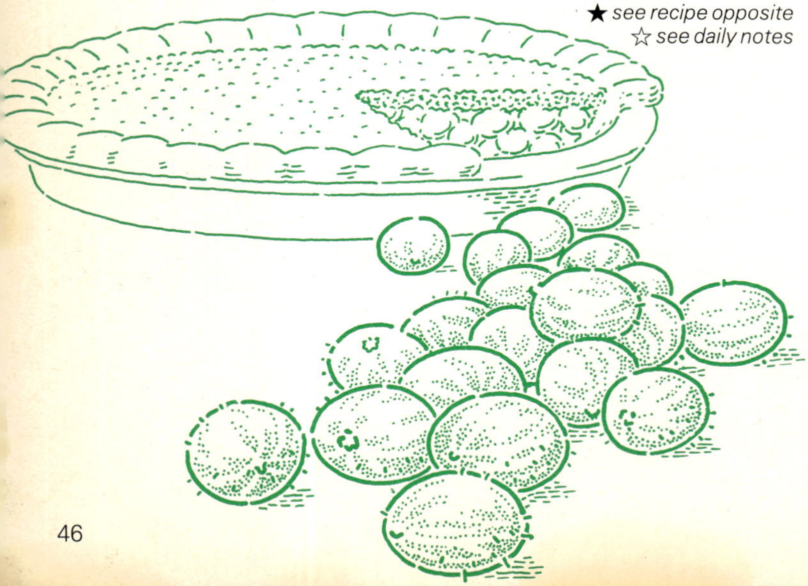

Gooseberry Flapjack Tart

Monday

Moist meat sandwiches: chop leftover meat and add shredded lettuce, grated raw carrot and salad cream to make the filling. **Pack:** spoon. **For tomorrow:** hard-boil eggs. Make Gooseberry Flapjack Tart.

Tuesday

Grill bacon rashers and remove rinds. Add with sliced tomatoes to fill roll. Egg and cress roll-ups, see page 43. **Pack:** fork. **For tomorrow:** prepare Gala Cheese Salad, see page 39. Make or buy orange mousse.

Wednesday

Pack: fork and spoon. **For tomorrow:** grill sausages. Prepare grated raw carrot and shredded cabbage for the sandwiches. Make Chocolate Nut Bars, see page 39.

Thursday

Make lower layer of double decker sandwiches with ham, top layer with grated raw carrot, raisins, shredded cabbage and salad cream, see page 41. **Pack:** fingers-only menu. **For tomorrow:** prepare Crispy Mackerel Salad.

Friday

Sprinkle the fresh fruit mixture with castor sugar if necessary. **Pack:** fork and spoon.

Crispy Mackerel Salad

When lettuce gets boring, crisp up appetites by using summer vegetables this way. Pack an individual portion in a plastic container and serve the remainder for lunch or supper.

For 4 portions

2 lb (1 kg) broad beans
3 tablespoons French dressing
4 slices bread from a large white loaf
2 oz (50 g) butter
2 tablespoons oil
1 rounded tablespoon chopped parsley
1 (7.05 oz, 200 g) can mackerel steak
Tomato
Cucumber

1. Shell the beans and cook in boiling salted water until tender, about 10 minutes. Drain and place in a bowl with French dressing; leave to cool.
2. Remove the crusts from the bread, cut the bread into cubes and fry in butter and oil, mixed, until golden brown; stir in parsley.
3. Drain liquor from mackerel, remove skin and lightly flake the fish. Mix fish, beans and bread cubes together.
4. Slice the tomato and cucumber and add to salad.

Gooseberry Flapjack Tart

The chewy flapjack on this tart makes a few early gooseberries go a long way.

For 6 portions

Pastry:

6 oz (150 g) plain flour
½ level teaspoon salt
3 oz (75 g) margarine and lard, mixed

Filling and topping:

12 oz (300 g) gooseberries
4 level tablespoons golden syrup
1½ oz (30 g) soft brown sugar
1½ oz (30 g) margarine
3 oz (75 g) rolled (porridge) oats

1. Prepare a moderately hot oven (400°F, 200°C, Gas Mark 6).
2. Place flour and salt in a bowl, add the fats, cut into small pieces, and rub in with fingertips until mixture resembles fine breadcrumbs. Add about 2 tablespoons of cold water and mix with a fork to form a firm dough. Turn out on to a floured surface; knead lightly until dough is smooth.
3. Roll out pastry into a 9 in circle and line an 8 in ovenproof pie plate. Press lightly on to plate, do not trim. Tuck under pastry round edge. Using the back of a knife, cut edge to form flakes. Press the prongs of a fork on to pastry rim, then flute edge by lightly pressing edge with thumb and drawing back of knife towards the centre.
4. Top and tail gooseberries and spread over the pastry. Measure the golden syrup carefully into a small saucepan. Add the sugar and margarine to the saucepan and heat gently until margarine has melted. Stir in rolled oats, then spread mixture over gooseberries.
5. Place tart on a baking sheet; bake in the centre of the oven for 40 minutes or until golden brown on top.

SCHOOL CHILDREN

Monday

☆ Chunky cooked meat and lettuce rolls

Fruit yogurt

Crisps

Chocolate nuts and raisins

Tuesday

☆ Sausages and spicy dip

☆ Cream cheese roll-ups

Fresh fruit

Jam tart

Wednesday

★ Leicester Meat Loaf

Wholemeal roll and butter

Tomato and cucumber salad

☆ Fruity mousse

Chocolate bar

Thursday

Scotch eggs

☆ Crunchy vegetable sandwiches

★ Apricot Flan

★ see recipe opposite
☆ see daily notes

Friday

☆ Kipper Loaf

Crusty French bread and butter

Fresh fruit

Peanuts

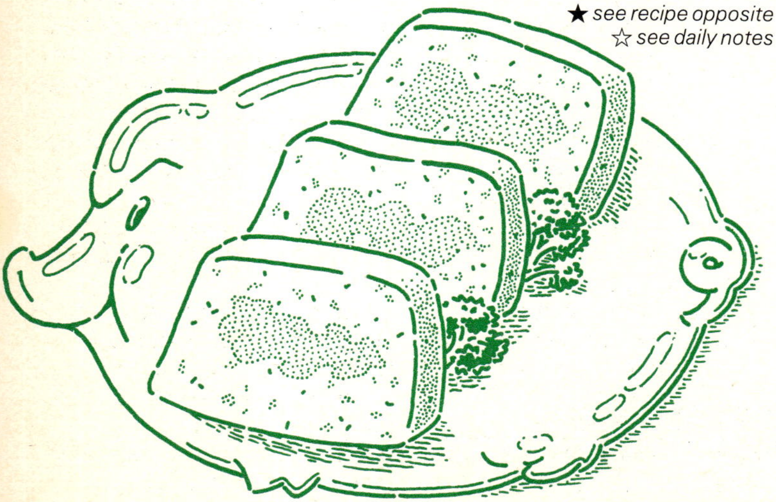

Leicester Meat Loaf

Monday

Chunky cooked meat and lettuce rolls: chop cooked meat left over from Sunday, fill rolls with the meat, lettuce and some mayonnaise for moisture. **Pack:** spoon. **For tomorrow:** grill sausages.

Tuesday

Make cold cooked sausages more fun by putting a small amount of favourite relish in a small plastic container. Cream cheese roll-ups, see page 43. **Pack:** a fingers-only menu. **For tomorrow:** make Leicester Meat Loaf. Prepare salad. Make fruity mousse: in a small saucepan melt a jelly in ¼ pint (5 fl oz) water, leave to cool. Whisk a small can of evaporated milk, then whisk in the cooled jelly slowly.

Wednesday

Pack: knife, fork and spoon. **For tomorrow:** make or buy Scotch eggs. Grate raw carrot, shred lettuce and mix with raisins and salad cream for crunchy vegetable sandwiches. Make Apricot Flan.

Thursday

Cut Scotch eggs in half for easier eating. **Pack:** spoon. **For tomorrow:** make Kipper Loaf, see page 41.

Friday

Make an interesting mixture of soft fresh fruit in a plastic container. Add dried apricots, if liked. **Pack:** knife and fork.

Leicester Meat Loaf

Wrap portions in foil.

For 6 to 8 portions

1 small onion
4 rashers streaky bacon
5 oz (125 g) Leicester cheese
1 lb (½ kg) pork sausagemeat
½ level teaspoon dried thyme
2 level tablespoons freshly chopped parsley
4 oz (100 g) fresh white breadcrumbs
1 level teaspoon salt, pepper

1. Prepare a moderate oven (375°F, 190°C, Gas Mark 5). Grease a 2 pint capacity loaf tin, line base with greaseproof paper; grease paper.
2. Peel and finely chop onion. Remove rind and bone from bacon; chop bacon. Cube cheese.
3. Place bacon in a small saucepan, heat gently until the fat begins to run, add onion and fry for about 4 minutes.
4. Place bacon and onion in a large bowl with sausagemeat, thyme, chopped parsley, breadcrumbs, salt and pepper. Mix well with a fork.
5. Spread half the mixture in the tin, making a dip along the centre. Fill the dip with cheese cubes; spread the rest of the mixture over the top to enclose cheese. Cover tin with foil.
6. Place tin in a roasting tin half filled with water. Bake in centre of oven for 1 hour. Remove from roasting tin and cool in tin for about 1 hour. Invert on to a serving dish, remove paper and leave to cool completely; chill.

Apricot Flan

You can use tinned apricot halves for this flan instead of fresh ones. Using canned ones, omit step 3 of the recipe. Wrap an individual portion in foil or put in a small plastic container.

For 4 to 6 portions

1 8 in baked pastry flan case

Lemon custard:
2 level tablespoons custard powder
2 level tablespoons granulated sugar
½ pint (10 fl oz) milk
Finely-grated rind of 1 lemon

½ lb (225 g) fresh apricots
2 oz (50 g) granulated sugar
1 level tablespoon flaked or shredded almonds

1. Place flan case on a plate.
2. To make filling: blend custard powder, sugar and a little of the measured milk in a small saucepan. Add the remaining milk, bring to boil, stirring, and cook for 1 minute. Remove pan from heat and stir in the finely-grated lemon rind. Pour into the flan case; leave to cool.
3. Wash, halve and stone the apricots. Place ¼ pint (5 fl oz) water and 2 oz sugar in a medium-sized saucepan; stir over a low heat, until sugar has dissolved. Bring to boil, add the apricots, cover with a lid, reduce heat and simmer for 8 to 10 minutes, until tender.
4. Carefully lift apricot halves out of the syrup, using a draining spoon. Dry on kitchen paper, then arrange over custard in the flan case, rounded sides upwards.
5. To make glaze: bring the apricot syrup in saucepan to boil and boil quickly until reduced to about 3 tablespoons; brush over the apricots.
6. Toast almonds; sprinkle over the apricots; chill.

SLIMMERS

Monday

☆ Rosy hard-boiled egg

Mixed salad

Orange mousse

Tuesday

Tuna salad

★ Strawberry and Orange Cups

Wednesday

Seasoned lean pork chop

Three Cs salad; cress chicory and cucumber

Edam cheese

Thursday

★ Cucumber Cocktail Soup

Lean ham slices

Banana

★ see recipe opposite
☆ see daily notes

Note: all accompanied by crispbread spread thinly with poly-unsaturated fat.

Friday

Chicken salad

Fresh raspberries

Strawberry and Orange Cups

Monday

Hard boil an egg the night before, sprinkle with paprika. Prepare salad ingredients also the night before and put on a plastic plate covered with cling film. Save and pack an extra portion of orange mousse if making one for the family, or take a frozen one out of the freezer. **Pack:** fork and spoon, crispbread. **For tomorrow:** prepare the tuna salad and some Strawberry and Orange Cups.

Tuesday

Pack: fork and spoon, crispbread. **For tomorrow:** prepare the Three Cs salad, cook an extra pork chop with the family supper, slice or cube Edam cheese and wrap in cling film.

Wednesday

Season the pork chop. **Pack:** knife and fork, crispbread. **For tomorrow:** prepare the Cucumber Cocktail Soup and keep in the fridge.

Thursday

Put the iced soup in a vacuum flask. **Pack:** knife and fork, crispbread. **For tomorrow:** Cook a piece of chicken, or use leftovers, dice and mix with a variety of salad ingredients. Keep in the fridge over night.

Friday

Put the fresh raspberries into a container with a lid so they don't stain the rest of the lunchbox. **Pack:** fork and spoon, crispbread.

Strawberry and Orange Cups

Wrap the individual cups in cling film for easy transporting. Store in the fridge.

For 4 portions

4 oz (100 g) strawberries
2 large oranges
Liquid sweetener, optional

1. Wash the strawberries and reserve 4 for decoration. Hull the remainder, cut into quarters and place in a bowl.
2. Scrub the oranges; cut each in half horizontally. Using a sharp or serrated knife, cut around each orange half between flesh and pith. Holding the orange over the strawberries in the bowl, cut between segments. Carefully lift out segments with a spoon and lightly mix with the strawberries. Add a few drops of liquid sweetener to taste, if desired. Remove pith and reserve orange shells.
3. Divide fruit equally between the four orange shells and top each with one of the reserved strawberries.

Cucumber Cocktail Soup

A delicious chilled soup for summer meals. This will keep for a few days in the fridge.

For 4 portions

1 small onion
Half a medium-sized cucumber (about 6 oz, 175 g)
1 teaspoon oil
¼ level teaspoon dried basil
Celery salt
1 chicken stock cube
½ pint (10 fl oz) boiling water
1 pint (20 fl oz) canned tomato juice
Half a small bay leaf
1 teaspoon Worcester sauce
Salt and pepper

1. Peel the onion; chop finely. Dice the cucumber finely.
2. Heat the oil in a medium-sized saucepan. Add the onion, diced cucumber, basil and a shake of celery salt. Fry gently over a low heat for 2 minutes, stirring all the time.
3. Dissolve the stock cube in boiling water. Make up to 1 pint with some of the tomato juice; add to saucepan, with bay leaf, Worcester sauce, ¼ level teaspoon salt and a shake of pepper. Bring to boil, stirring; simmer for 5 minutes. Leave to cool. Chill the remaining tomato juice.
4. Pour soup into a chilled bowl and add remaining tomato juice; remove bay leaf. Taste and add more salt and pepper, if necessary. Leave in fridge until needed, skimming off any oil with kitchen paper before using.

Monday

Chopped cooked meat

☆ Summer vegetable salad

Lemony fresh peaches

Tuesday

Hard-boiled egg

★ Slimline Salad

Fresh pineapple with cottage cheese

Wednesday

Chicken cube salad

★ Fruit Fool

Thursday

☆ Smoked mackerel with savoury salad

Natural yogurt

Fresh strawberries

Friday

Chilled consommé

★ Summer Tossed Salad

Edam cheese

★ see recipe opposite
☆ see daily notes
Note: all accompanied by crispbread spread thinly with poly-unsaturated fat.

Slimline Salad

Monday

Chop up slices of cold meat from the weekend joint. Save some mixed veg from the weekend and put in a container. Slice the fresh peaches and sprinkle with lemon juice. **Pack:** fork and spoon, crispbread. **For tomorrow:** hard-boil egg, make Slimline Salad.

Tuesday

Slice the hard-boiled egg. Cut a couple of slices of fresh pineapple and either mix with the cottage cheese or carry separately. **Pack:** fork and spoon, crispbread. **For tomorrow:** cube cooked chicken and mix with sliced peppers, tomatoes and cucumber. Make Fruit Fool.

Wednesday

Pack: fork and spoon, crispbread. **For tomorrow:** flake the smoked mackerel, hard-boil egg, shred white cabbage.

Thursday

Slice the hard-boiled egg and mix in with the fish and cabbage or carry in separate containers. Put the strawberries in a container. **Pack:** fork and spoon, crispbread. **For tomorrow:** make or buy consommé. Prepare the Summer Tossed Salad and cover with cling film. Cube and cover Edam cheese.

Friday

Pour the chilled consommé into a vacuum flask. Take some salad dressing in a sealed container. **Pack:** fork, crispbread.

Slimline Salad

The vegetables and dressing can be prepared in advance and stored in the fridge for up to two days. Non-slimmers would enjoy it too.

For 4 to 6 portions

12 oz (350 g) carrots
1 medium-sized green pepper
8 oz (225 g) broad beans
Salt
1/4 pint (5 fl oz) natural yogurt
1 rounded tablespoon chopped mint
Pepper

1. Scrape the carrots; cut into 3 in sticks.
2. Cut the pepper in half lengthwise, discard seeds, core and white pith; slice.
3. Shell the beans; cook beans and carrots in boiling, salted water for about 7 to 10 minutes. Drain and cool quickly.
4. Mix the vegetables; pile into individual containers or a serving dish.
5. Mix together the yogurt, mint and a little salt and pepper. Dress the salad just before serving.

Fruit Fool

Use just one or a mixture of fruit to make this refreshing dish. Blackberries, gooseberries or rhubarb will need cooking first.

For 1 portion

Small cupful of fruit (see above)
1 teaspoon dried skimmed milk
Few drops of liquid sweetener, optional

Place the fruit, dried skimmed milk and liquid sweetener in a liquidiser goblet. Add a little cold water. Run the machine until the mixture is smooth. Pack in a well-sealed plastic container.

Summer Tossed Salad

A nourishing and refreshing dish. Packed in individual containers it can be kept in the fridge for a few days.

For 4 portions

12 oz (350 g) cottage cheese
4 sticks celery
3/4 lb (350 g) lean ham
2 red-skinned eating apples
Small bunch of radishes

Place the cottage cheese in a mixing bowl, wash and slice the celery, slice the ham in strips, core and chop the apples; wash and slice the radishes and mix all together with the cottage cheese.

FAMILIES ON THE MOVE

Taking it with you – foodwise – makes sense on family journeys. It's cheaper, you can take the kind of food you and the family enjoy and it's more convenient as you can eat it when and where you please. The top two menus on this page are for 'mess-free' meals, easy-to-carry, that you can eat in the train, on the ferry or any convenient spot on your way to, say, a museum or exhibition. The lower two menus are for slightly more sedate meals – that is when you're on a long journey, perhaps to visit relations, but you're prepared to actually stop the car and spread yourself a little.

On the move

Filled rolls *(see opposite)*

Cold sausages and spicy dip *(see page 21)*

Tomato and cucumber wedges

Spicy fruit cake

Apples

On the move

Double decker sandwiches *(see page 41)*

Scotch eggs

Individual fruit pies

Cheese and biscuits

When you stop

Breaded lamb chops

Corn and sultana salad

Cold new minty potatoes

Bakewell tart

Fresh fruit in season

When you stop

Tomato soup in flask

Chicken legs

Cheese-filled celery

Individual trifles

Crisps and nuts

HOW TO PACK

on-the-move meals

The secret packaging ingredient with meals like this is not to use bulky containers – who wants to spend the rest of the day carting them around empty. Instead use disposable packaging (like foil) and put everything in a fold-up type bag that you can put in your pocket afterwards. For drinks with these kinds of meals buy cans or cartons and maybe take straws. If you want a hot drink, be extravagant and buy cups of tea or coffee on the train, ferry or at the exhibition. And remember to take something to spread on laps and clean up sticky fingers – paper napkins or sheets of kitchen roll.

when-you-stop-meals

You can pack these in a more expansive way – in flasks, polythene containers and so on. But don't forget to take plates, forks, knives, spoons, cups for soup and paper napkins or pieces of kitchen roll. If you don't run to a picnic hamper or basket, pack everything away in a cardboard box from the grocers, or your polythene washing basket. And try to pack the food in the order in which you'll be eating it.

AND WHEN YOU'VE FINISHED... throw all your litter into a bin.

OVER 60 IDEAS FOR SANDWICH AND ROLL FILLINGS

Hard cheese, grated or sliced with:

Horseradish
Chopped dates
Tomato ketchup
Tomato or cucumber slices
Mustard
Jelly mint sauce
Sandwich spread
Radish
Lemon sprinkled apple slices
Sweet pickle or chutney

Cream or cottage cheese with:

Chopped mint
Mixed chopped nuts
Pineapple
Chives
Sweetcorn and pimento

Egg with:

A touch of curry paste
Watercress
Mayonnaise and chives
Mayonnaise and celery
Chopped with liver pâté
Mayonnaise and watercress

Peanut butter with:

Mashed banana
Grated cheese and sliced tomato
Salad
Jam (some kids love it)

Fish:

Tuna with salad cream and chopped celery
Sardines, mashed with cucumber slices
Sardines with tomato ketchup
Shrimps and parsley
Dressed crab and mayonnaise
Salmon and cucumber

Liver sausage with:

Watercress
Lettuce
Cucumber
Tomato
Coleslaw

Salami with:

Salad
Mayonnaise

Ham with:

Pickle
Cheese

Cold meats, chopped or sliced with:

Shredded lettuce and salad cream
Tomato chutney
Coleslaw

Sausages, sliced with:

Grated onion
Sweetcorn relish
Tomato ketchup

Chicken with:

Mayonnaise
Corn relish
Raw mushroom
Sliced new potatoes and chopped parsley

All kinds of pastes with:

Salad
Tomato
Cucumber
Cress

Yeast extract with:

Cress
Tomato

Vegetables:

Chopped celery and apple with salad cream
Grated raw carrot and raisins
Sandwich spread

Menu 1

★ Viennese Split

Frankfurter Salad Kebabs *(see page 37)*

★ Fresh Raspberry and Orange Mousse

Fresh fruit

Assorted plain and sweet biscuits

Menu 2

Potted Bacon Spread *(see page 87)*

Baked Chicken Roll *(see page 63)*

Wholemeal rolls

★ Garden Salad Platter

★ Apple Cheesecake

★ *see recipe opposite*

Viennese Split

For 4 portions
1 Vienna loaf
Butter
Lettuce
4 oz (100 g) salami, sliced
1 small carton coleslaw

1. Cut the loaf into 4 equal-sized pieces; cut each piece twice along the length, taking care not to cut through to the other side. Spread cut edges with butter.
2. Wash the lettuce; tear into small pieces. Remove skin from salami and place in the bottom cut. Place the lettuce and the coleslaw in the top layer of the bread.

Raspberry and Orange Mousse

For 4 portions
2 medium-sized oranges
½ lb (200 g) raspberries
2 oz (50 g) granulated sugar
½ oz (1 envelope) gelatine
1 small packet dessert topping mix
Milk

1. Scrub oranges, reserve one for decoration, grate rind and squeeze juice from remaining orange.
2. Reserving a few raspberries for decoration, place the remainder in a medium-sized saucepan with orange rind, juice, ¼ pint (5 fl oz) water and sugar.
3. Bring to boil, cover and simmer for 5 minutes.
4. Make a purée by rubbing the raspberries through a sieve with a wooden spoon, or blend in a liquidiser until smooth.
5. Place the gelatine in a basin with 3 tablespoons of cold

water; place in a saucepan of hot, but not boiling water. Stir until gelatine has dissolved.
6. Stir the gelatine into the raspberry purée, leave until cold. Make up the dessert topping as directed on the packet, using milk.
7. Whisk the purée into the dessert topping until evenly blended. Pour into a suitably sized plastic container; chill until set.
8. Cut 6 thin slices from the remaining orange; cut each slice from centre to edge. Arrange in twists on the top of the mousse with the reserved raspberries to decorate.

Garden Salad Platter

For 4 portions
1 lettuce
2 carrots
1 green pepper
8 radishes
2 tomatoes

1. Discard the outer leaves of lettuce, wash lettuce well, shake dry and arrange leaves in a large plastic container. Scrub carrots and grate. Wash pepper; cut off stalk and remove seeds and pith. Cut pepper into rings.
2. Wash the radishes and tomatoes; slice tomatoes thinly.
3. Arrange the prepared vegetables in the container with the lettuce.

Apple Cheesecake

Makes 4
Pastry:
5 oz (150 g) plain flour
3 oz (75 g) margarine
2 rounded teaspoons castor sugar
Filling:
1 large cooking apple (about ½ lb, 225 g)
Castor sugar
½ level teaspoon ground cinnamon
1 oz (25 g) margarine
1 level teaspoon grated lemon rind
¼ lb (100 g) curd cheese
1 standard egg

1. Prepare a moderate oven (375°F, 190°C, Gas Mark 5).
2. Place the flour in a bowl. Add the margarine and rub in until mixture resembles fine breadcrumbs. Stir in 2 rounded teaspoons castor sugar. Add about 1 tablespoon cold water and mix with a fork, to form a firm dough.
3. Turn out on to a floured board and knead lightly. Cut into 4 equal-sized pieces. Roll out each piece and line 4 (3½ in) individual pie tins.
4. Peel and core the apple. Cut into small pieces and place in a basin, with 1 rounded tablespoon castor sugar and cinnamon; mix well. Divide apple mixture evenly between pastry cases.
5. Melt the margarine in a small saucepan over a low heat. Remove from heat and stir in 2 oz (50 g) castor sugar, lemon rind and curd cheese; mix together. Separate egg; place white in a clean, grease-free basin and beat yolk into cheese mixture. Whisk egg white until stiff, but not dry; fold into cheese mixture. Divide mixture evenly between tins and level tops with back of spoon.
6. Bake in centre of oven for 35 to 40 minutes, until filling is well risen and golden brown. Leave to cool completely in tins.

HOW TO PACK MENU 1

Viennese Split – wrap in foil or cling film.
Frankfurter Salad Kebabs – place in a large, shallow plastic container and cover with foil.
Raspberry and Orange Mousse – make in a plastic container with a lid.
Fresh fruit – if it's tough, apples, bananas, put in plastic bags. Place more fragile fruit in a plastic container.
Biscuits – place in a plastic container with a lid.

HOW TO PACK MENU 2

Potted Bacon Spread – cover individual foil dishes.
Baked Chicken Roll – pack whole roll, or individual pieces in foil or cling film.
Crunchy brown rolls – butter and pack in plastic bags.
Garden Salad Platter – make in a plastic container with a lid.
Apple Cheesecake – put on small plates and wrap in foil.

CHECKLIST: HAVE YOU PACKED?-

★ Cutlery
★ Paper or plastic plates
★ Paper napkins
★ Salt and pepper
★ Drinks and cups
★ Sugar and milk
★ Something to sit on
★ Bags for the 'dirties'

CHILDREN'S PICNIC PARTIES

Menu 1

Golden chicken bites *(see page 35)*

★ Cheesy roll-ups

Birthday cake

★ Mallow Chocolate Crunch

Fruit salad

Potato puffs, cheese straws etc

Menu 2

Variety of sandwiches *(see page 55)*

Malty fruit loaf and butter

Sausages on sticks

★ Chocolate and Orange Allsorts

Birthday cake

Fruit Jelly

Nuts, crisps and fruit

★ *see recipes right*

Cheesy Roll-ups

Makes 8

8 large slices brown bread
2 oz (50 g) Danish blue cheese
1 oz (25 g) butter, softened
Pepper
2 to 3 sticks celery

1. Remove crusts from bread.
2. Crumble the cheese and place in a basin with butter and a good shake of pepper. Beat together until smooth.
3. Roll out the bread slices with a rolling pin. Spread each slice generously with cheese mixture. Cut celery sticks to fit length of bread. Place one stick on one end of each slice of bread and roll up firmly.

Mallow Chocolate Crunch

Makes 12 pieces

¾ lb (350 g) plain chocolate digestive biscuits
1 (4.34 oz, 123 g) packet marshmallows
1 oz (25 g) margarine
2 tablespoons milk
1 level tablespoon cocoa

1. Place the biscuits between 2 sheets of greaseproof paper; crush finely with a rolling pin.
2. Reserve 6 marshmallows; cut the remaining marshmallows into small pieces and place in a medium-sized saucepan, with margarine, milk and cocoa. Heat gently, stirring, until marshmallows have melted.
3. Add biscuit crumbs to melted mixture; mix well. Turn out the biscuit mixture into a shallow, 7 in square cake tin.
4. Mark top into 12 portions. Cut reserved marshmallows in halves. Press each half into centre of each portion; leave to cool. Cover tin with foil or cling film.

Chocolate and Orange Allsorts

Makes about 18 biscuits

Biscuits:
1 small orange
9 oz (225 g) plain flour
6 oz (150 g) butter or margarine
3 oz (75 g) castor sugar
2 level tablespoons cocoa

Icing:
6 oz (150 g) icing sugar
Orange food colouring
3 tablespoons orange juice

1. Prepare a moderate oven (350°F, 180°C, Gas Mark 4). Grease an 11 in by 7 in shallow oblong tin.
2. Scrub the orange; grate rind and squeeze juice. Place the flour in a bowl. Add the fat and rub in until the mixture resembles fine breadcrumbs. Add castor sugar; mix well.
3. Place half the mixture in another bowl and stir in the cocoa. Mix the orange rind and a few drops of orange colouring in a small basin; add to other half of mixture and mix well.
4. Sprinkle the chocolate-flavoured mixture evenly over prepared tin. Repeat with orange-flavoured mixture.
5. Bake in the centre of the oven for about 35 minutes until just beginning to colour at the edges. Leave to cool in the tin 5 minutes, then cut into 4 along length and into 6 diagonally to form diamonds and triangles. Leave in tin until completely cold.
6. Ice just before you want to eat them. Beat icing ingredients until smooth and glossy. Pour over biscuits in tin; leave until set.

Menu 1

Chicken soup

Barbecued meats with sauce

★ Cheesy Frankfurters

Mixed vegetable salad

★ Caribbean Banana Bake

Menu 2

Bacon chowder

Lamb rib chops

Jacket potatoes topped with tangy mustard sauce

Courgette, pepper and onion salad with French dressing

★ Spicy Dampers with Jam Sauce

★ see recipes right

Cheesy Frankfurters

Make these the day before and store, covered, in the fridge.

Makes 8

2 processed cheese slices
8 frankfurters
8 rashers streaky bacon
8 long, soft rolls

1. Cut each cheese slice into 4 strips. Cut a slit through frankfurters to within about ¼ in of each end.
2. Place a strip of cheese inside each slit of frankfurters.
3. Remove rind and bone from bacon. Stretch each rasher with the back of a knife. Wrap a rasher of bacon around each frankfurter, tucking ends of bacon into the slits.
4. Grease grill rack. Grill frankfurters over hot embers of a wood fire or barbeque charcoal, until the bacon is cooked. Serve immediately in long rolls, which have been gently warmed beside the fire.

Caribbean Banana Bake

Make the orange butter to serve with the bananas the day before.

Makes 6

Orange butter
2 oz (50 g) butter
2 oz (50 g) soft light brown sugar
1 medium-sized orange
6 firm ripe bananas

1. Cream the butter and sugar together in a bowl. Scrub the orange and grate rind.
2. Cut the orange in half and squeeze juice. Beat orange rind and 2 teaspoons orange juice into the butter mixture.
3. Place the bananas, in skins, on the grill rack over hot embers of a wood fire or barbeque charcoal. Grill until skins turn black on the underside. Turn and grill on other side, until skins turn black and bananas feel soft.
4. When bananas are cooked, cut skin from one side of each with a sharp-pointed knife. Serve hot, with orange butter.

Spicy Dampers with Jam Sauce

If giving a large party, serve different flavoured jam sauces, and perhaps some honey, with the dampers. For cooking you will need 8 thick sticks, each about 18 in long, freshly cut from the hedgerow.

Makes 8

Jam sauce:
3 tablespoons apricot jam

Dampers:
8 oz (225 g) self-raising flour
½ level teaspoon salt
½ level teaspoon mixed spice
1 rounded tablespoon castor sugar

1. Place the apricot jam and 2 tablespoons of water in a small saucepan. Heat gently. Place in a warmed dish and keep warm.
2. Place the flour, salt, mixed spice and castor sugar in a bowl. Add cold water to form a firm dough. Knead lightly.
3. Scrub the ends of sticks. Divide dough into 8 equal pieces and roll each piece into an 8 in strip. Coil strips around end of sticks. Cook over hot embers of a wood fire or barbeque charcoal until lightly browned. Pull the dampers off the sticks and serve immediately with sauce.

SPECIAL OCCASION PICNICS

Menu for 4

★ Gaspacho

Assorted pâtés

French bread and butter

Cold roast duck and stuffing

Potato and radish salad

Coleslaw and pepper salad

★ Blackcurrant Citrus Cups

Cheese platter and biscuits

Menu for 6

Chilled Cucumber Soup

Salmon mousse

★ Chicken and Sweetcorn Salad

German sausage platter

Tomato salad

Fruit Tart

Brown rolls and butter

★ *see recipes opposite*

Gaspacho

For 4 portions
1 lb (½ kg) ripe tomatoes
1 medium-sized lemon
1 clove garlic
1 level teaspoon salt
1 medium-sized onion
1 medium-sized red pepper
1 medium-sized green pepper
Half a cucumber
Oil
½ pint (10 fl oz) tomato juice
Pepper
2 slices white bread

1. Peel and chop tomatoes; reserve 3 tablespoons and place in a bowl. Squeeze lemon juice.
2. Peel the clove of garlic and place on a saucer with the salt. Using a round-ended knife, rub salt against garlic to crush clove. Peel and chop onion. Cut the peppers in halves lengthwise; discard seeds, cores and white pith; cut into small dice. Cut cucumber into ½ in dice.
3. Place half of each vegetable, except onion, in small serving bowls and reserve. Heat 1 tablespoon of oil in a medium-sized saucepan, add garlic, onion, remaining peppers and cucumber. Cook gently for 5 minutes to soften. Add to tomatoes and press through a sieve into a bowl, then strain.
4. Add the tomato juice, 3 tablespoons of oil, lemon juice and a shake of pepper; mix together, taste and add more seasoning if necessary. Pour soup into a tureen; chill.
5. Prepare a hot grill; toast slices of bread and cut into cubes. Place bread in a small bowl. Serve soup with accompanying bowls of tomato, red pepper, green pepper, cucumber and cubes of toasted bread.

Blackcurrant Citrus Cups

For 4 portions

4 medium-sized oranges
1 blackcurrant-flavoured jelly

1. Place a large nylon sieve over a large basin. Cut a ¾ in slice from the bottom of each orange and reserve slices for 'lids'.
2. Hold each orange over the sieve. Using a sharp or serrated knife, cut flesh from inside orange, taking care not to pierce the shell. Scoop out any remaining flesh and pith with a teaspoon. Place orange flesh in sieve. Reserve the orange shells.
3. Using a wooden spoon, press orange flesh firmly, to release juice; discard pulp. Pour juice into a measuring jug; make up to ¾ pint (15 fl oz) with water, if necessary.
4. Cut the blackcurrant jelly into small pieces. Place in a saucepan, with 4 tablespoons juice. Heat gently; stir until jelly has dissolved. Remove from heat and add remaining juice; return to jug and leave until almost set.
5. Place the orange shells, cut sides uppermost, on a small tray. Pour jelly into shells, and leave in fridge until set. When set, replace lids and wrap each orange in cling film or foil. Place oranges in an upright position in a plastic container with a lid. Store in fridge until ready to leave for picnic. Serve with canned cream, if desired.

Chicken and Sweetcorn Salad

For 6 portions

2 cooked chicken portions
1 small onion
1 small clove of garlic
Salt and pepper
1 oz (25 g) margarine
3 oz (75 g) long-grain rice
1 (7 oz, 198 g) can sweetcorn
½ medium-sized red pepper
2 rounded tablespoons thick, mild mayonnaise
1 small lettuce
Lemon juice

1. Remove skin from the chicken portions; cut away flesh; cut flesh into small pieces. Place skin and bones in a small saucepan; cover with water. Bring to boil; cover and simmer for 15 minutes.
2. Peel and chop the onion. Peel the clove of garlic and place on a saucer with a little salt. With a round-ended knife, rub salt against garlic, to crush.
3. Melt the margarine in a large saucepan; add the crushed garlic, onion and chicken and fry gently for 5 minutes. Add the rice; fry until rice has absorbed fat. Add ½ pint (10 fl oz) hot chicken stock; bring to boil. Reduce heat; cover and simmer for 20 minutes, stirring occasionally, until rice is tender and stock absorbed; cool.
4. Drain the can of sweetcorn. Cut 6 slices off the red pepper and reserve. Finely chop remaining pepper and add to chicken mixture, with mayonnaise, sweetcorn, some salt and pepper; mix together.
5. Remove and discard the outer leaves of lettuce; wash the lettuce well. Shred finely and divide equally between 6 individual plastic containers. Sprinkle lettuce with salt and lemon juice. Divide chicken mixture between containers.
6. Garnish each salad with reserved slices of red pepper. Cover with a lid or foil.

HOW TO PACK

Packing a special picnic takes a little more time and trouble, but it is the extra touches that give it the air of luxury.

The great secret is to carry the trimmings and accompaniments separately so that they can be added at the last minute. And everything should be kept as cool as possible.

Make notes on things to take to make the picnic special, such as a pretty tablecloth, paper napkins, china plates or alternatively patterned paper ones, bottle of chilled wine, etc.

Cold soups: chill well before setting off and pour into large wide-necked vacuum flasks.

Cold duck or other poultry: chill well and carry in a high-domed plastic container, add the orange slices or other trimmings around the dish at the last moment.

Sausage platter: buy a selection of sausages and ham. Mild cheeses make a delicious accompaniment.

Pâtés: if these are bought or made at home, an assortment in small dishes makes serving easy and gives variety. These are best well chilled.

Salads: always choose good crisp lettuce; make up other salads at home and pack them into attractive containers from which you can serve.

Dressing: make up at home and carry in a jar or plastic pot with a tight-fitting lid.

Fruit flan or tart: place on a serving plate and cover with foil, or pack in a plastic cake carrier. Alternatively return it to the flan ring or tin in which it was made, place on a serving plate and wrap carefully in foil.

MEN AND WOMEN AT WORK

Monday

Pâté and tomato roll

Egg mayonnaise and lettuce sandwich

Grape and orange salad

Tuesday

Pork pie

☆ Creamy cheese and onion roll-ups

☆ Dutch apple stew

Wednesday

★ Baked Chicken Roll

Coleslaw

Wholemeal scones

Fresh fruit purée

Thursday

Scotch eggs

☆ Cheesy baked beans

Tomato salad

★ Ginger Teabread

★ see recipe opposite
☆ see daily notes

Friday

☆ Tasty tuna fish rolls

Cheese-filled celery sticks

Orange and banana salad

Baked Chicken Roll

Monday

All kinds of fresh and pre-packed pâtés are on sale for quick fillings. Mash hard-boiled egg with mayonnaise and seasoning. De-pip the grapes and peel and segment the orange. Sprinkle brown sugar over the top. **Pack:** spoon. **For tomorrow:** buy or make pork pie. Stew apple with cinnamon and sultanas or raisins.

Tuesday

Chop a pickled onion and add to the cream cheese for the roll-ups, see page 43. Cut pork pie into easy-to-eat slices. **Pack:** spoon. **For tomorrow:** make Baked Chicken Roll. Make or buy coleslaw. Make scones, purée seasonal fruit.

Wednesday

Open and butter scones, pack purée separately. **Pack:** two knives and a fork. **For tomorrow:** make or buy Scotch eggs. Make Ginger Teabread.

Thursday

Cut Scotch eggs in half. Grate cheese and wrap separately from the baked beans. **Pack:** fork. **For tomorrow:** prepare tuna fish filling.

Friday

Drain tuna fish, flake and add one or a mixture of: diced cucumber, tomato slices, chopped onions. Peel and slice banana, peel and segment orange. Sprinkle with lemon juice and sugar. **Pack:** spoon.

Baked Chicken Roll

When the roll is cool, cut into slices and wrap in foil or cling film. Serve remainder hot with vegetables for supper.

For 6 portions

1 medium-sized onion
4 chicken joints
Salt
½ pint (10 fl oz) boiling water
1 small (7 oz, 198 g) can sweetcorn with red and green peppers
Pepper
1 egg
1 Vienna loaf
2 oz (50 g) butter
1 level teaspoon garlic salt, optional

1. Prepare a moderate oven (350°F, 180°C, Gas Mark 4). To steam-boil chicken: peel the onion and place in a large saucepan with chicken joints, 1 level teaspoon salt and boiling water. Bring to boil, cover and simmer for 45 minutes. Remove from heat: leave to cool. Place the chicken on a board.
2. Remove the skin and bones from the chicken and cut the meat into small pieces. Place the meat in a bowl.
3. Drain the sweetcorn and add to bowl with ½ level teaspoon salt, a shake of pepper and egg. Mix thoroughly.
4. Cut along the length of the loaf, taking care not to cut through to the other side. Scoop out bread from centre of both halves; use to make breadcrumbs. Add 2 oz (50 g) breadcrumbs to the chicken mixture; mix together thoroughly.
5. Soften the butter, add garlic salt, if used, and beat thoroughly. Use the garlic butter to spread inside of loaf. Fill centre of loaf with chicken mixture; wrap loaf tightly in foil and bake in centre of oven for 30 minutes.

Ginger Teabread

Cut into slices, spread with butter and wrap in foil or cling film. It improves with keeping.

Makes 1 loaf

½ lb (200 g) mixed dried fruit
2 teaspoons stem ginger syrup
4 oz (100 g) granulated sugar
1 tea bag
2 pieces stem ginger
1 egg
1 level tablespoon black treacle
4 oz (100 g) wholemeal flour
4 oz (100 g) plain flour
2 level teaspoons baking powder

1. Place mixed dried fruit in a medium-sized saucepan; add stem ginger syrup, sugar and ¼ pint (5 fl oz) water. Bring to boil, stirring. Remove from heat; stir in the tea bag. Cover and leave for 5 minutes. Remove the tea bag; leave fruit mixture to cool.
2. Prepare a cool oven (325°F, 160°C, Gas Mark 3). Grease a 1 lb (1½ pint capacity) loaf tin.
3. Chop the stem ginger finely. Stir, with egg, into the fruit mixture. Measure treacle carefully and add to pan. Add flours and baking powder; mix well. Turn mixture into prepared tin; level top with back of spoon.
4. Bake in centre of oven for 1½ hours, until well risen and golden brown. Test by pressing with the fingers. If cooked, loaf should spring back and have begun to shrink from sides of tin. Leave in tin for 10 minutes, then turn out and leave to cool completely on a wire rack.

MEN AND WOMEN AT WORK

Monday

☆ Pineapple cheese and salad double deckers

Apple crumble

Tuesday

★ Crispy Beef Triangles

Green salad

Orange mousse

Wednesday

Chicken pasties

Coleslaw

Fruity sponge flan

Thursday

Liver sausage and pickle sandwiches

Egg and tomato salad

★ Cushioned Fruit Rolls

Friday

☆ Potted Pilchard Spread

Rye bread and butter

Fresh fruit

Fruit cake

★ *see recipe opposite*
☆ *see daily notes*

Crispy Beef Triangles

Monday

Bought small pots of cream cheese and pineapple are a tasty standy-by filler, see page 41 for how to make double decker sandwiches. For pud, use Sunday's leftovers. **Pack:** spoon. **For tomorrow:** make Crispy Beef Triangles. Prepare salad. Make or buy orange mousse.

Tuesday

Pack: knife, fork and spoon. **For tomorrow:** make or buy chicken pasties, coleslaw and fruity sponge flan.

Wednesday

Pack: knife, fork and spoon. **For tomorrow:** hard-boil egg(s) for salad. Make Cushioned Fruit Rolls.

Thursday

There are several kinds of liver sausage available, sample one you haven't tried before, or buy liver pâté. Add a favourite pickle. Chop tomato and hard-boiled eggs for salad and add mayonnaise. **Pack:** 2 forks. **For tomorrow:** make Potted Pilchard Spread, see page 73. Make or buy fruit cake.

Friday

Either peel, core and de-pip the fresh fruit as necessary and put in a container, or pack as it is. If rye bread isn't popular supply crispbread or rolls instead. **Pack:** knife.

Crispy Beef Triangles

When cold, wrap in foil or cling film for packed meals.

Makes 8 pasties

Filling:

1 (7 oz, 198 g) can corned beef
2 tablespoons tomato ketchup
Pepper

Pastry:

8 oz (200 g) plain flour
1 level teaspoon salt
3 oz (75 g) margarine
Oil for frying

1. To make filling: place the corned beef in a basin, add tomato ketchup and a shake of pepper and mash together.
2. Place the flour and salt in a bowl. Heat the margarine and 5 tablespoons of water in a small saucepan, when just boiling, add all at once to flour, mix to form a soft dough. Turn on to a floured surface and knead well.
3. Roll out pastry and trim to an oblong 8 in by 16 in. Cut pastry into 8 squares. Divide filling between pastry squares, spreading to about ½ in from edges in a triangular shape on one half of each pastry square. Brush edges with water and fold pastry over to form triangles Pinch edges together firmly.
4. Place pasties on a board, cover with cling film and chill for 30 minutes.
5. Pour about ½ in of oil into a large frying pan and heat; fry four pasties at a time for 3 minutes on each side until golden brown. Drain on kitchen paper.

Cushioned Fruit Rolls

Make this with any fruit purée.

Makes 10 to 12 slices

Filling:

1 lb (½ kg) plums
Sugar
6 trifle sponges
½ level teaspoon ground ginger

Cake mixture:

6 oz (150 g) self-raising flour
3 oz (75 g) margarine
1 oz (25 g) castor sugar
1 egg
Icing sugar

1. Wash the plums; place in a saucepan with sugar to taste. Stew for about 10 minutes until soft; pour contents of saucepan into a sieve over a bowl. Remove plums from sieve, remove stones and discard. Roughly chop plums and leave until cool. Crumble the sponge cake into plums; add ground ginger and mix well.
2. Prepare a moderately hot oven (375°F, 190°C, Gas Mark 5). Dust a baking sheet with a little flour.
3. Place flour and margarine into a bowl; cut fat into small pieces and rub in until mixture resembles fine breadcrumbs. Stir in 1 oz sugar; beat the egg, add to bowl; stir until mixture binds together. Knead lightly. Place dough on a lightly floured surface. Roll into a 10 in square.
4. Cut dough in half; place plum mixture down the centre of each piece. Dampen edges; from a long outside edge, carefully fold dough over filling and roll over to enclose with the join underneath. Press ends to seal; lift on to the baking sheet and repeat with the other half. Bake just above centre of oven for 15 to 20 minutes until firm to the touch and very pale golden.
5. Leave to cool for 5 minutes; carefully lift on to a cooling rack. When cold, cut diagonally into slices. Dust with icing sugar.

MEN AND WOMEN AT WORK

Monday

Veal and ham pie

☆ Red cabbage and currant salad

Trifle

Tuesday

★ Corn and Frankfurter Soup

Wholemeal roll and butter

Fruit pie

Wednesday

☆ Sausage and Apple Puff

Green salad

Flapjack or shortbread

Thursday

☆ Paprika chicken piece

☆ Chivey potato salad

Fruit crumble

★ *see recipe opposite*
☆ *see daily notes*

Friday

Tuna fish flan

Crusty French bread and butter

Celery sticks

★ Somerset Cider Cake

Somerset Cider Cake

Monday

Slice the raw red cabbage, add a few currants and coat with a French dressing. Use leftover pud, or a bought trifle. **Pack:** knife, fork and spoon. **For tomorrow:** make Corn and Frankfurter Soup. Make or buy fruit pie.

Tuesday

Pack: knife, fork and spoon. **For tomorrow:** make Sausage and Apple Puff, see page 75. Shred the lettuce and mix with cress, watercress, cucumber and green pepper. Make or buy flapjack or shortbread.

Wednesday

Take dressing or mayonnaise separately in a well-sealed container for the salad. **Pack:** knife and fork. **For tomorrow:** roast chicken piece. Boil potatoes for salad, slice while still warm and add mayonnaise. Make fruit crumble. **N.B. For Friday:** soak sultanas in cider for the Somerset Cider Cake.

Thursday

Sprinkle the chicken piece with paprika, add chopped chives to the potato salad. **Pack:** knife, fork and spoon. **For tomorrow:** make a tuna fish flan. Make Somerset Cider Cake.

Friday

Pack individual piece of fish flan in cling film. Cut the French bread into slices and butter before sandwiching together. **Pack:** fork.

Corn and Frankfurter Soup

A meal-by-itself soup. Pour into a wide-necked vacuum flask for taking to work.

For 4 portions

1 medium-sized onion
1 small or ½ a large cucumber
1 oz (25 g) margarine
1 oz (25 g) plain flour
1 (8 oz, 227 g) can frankfurter sausages
3 oz (75 g) Edam cheese, grated
½ pint (10 fl oz) boiling water
½ pint (10 fl oz) milk
1 large (11½ oz, 326 g) can sweetcorn niblets
1 small (8 oz, 227 g) can tomatoes
Salt and pepper

1. Peel and finely chop the onion. Dice the cucumber. Melt margarine in a medium-sized saucepan, add the onion and cucumber and fry gently for 5 to 10 minutes, without browning. Add flour and cook for a further 2 minutes, stirring from time to time.
2. Cut the frankfurters into ¼ in slices. Grate the cheese. Add boiling water to pan with milk, sweetcorn, tomatoes, frankfurter pieces, grated cheese, salt and a shake of pepper. Heat gently for 5 to 10 minutes, without boiling, until cheese has melted.

Somerset Cider Cake

A lovely, satisfying fruit cake. Store for up to two weeks in an airtight tin. It freezes well too, cut into individual portions interleafed with plastic tissue. The sultanas need to be soaked overnight in the cider.

Makes about 30 slices

1¼ lb (500 g) sultanas
½ pint (10 fl oz) sweet cider
1½ lb (600 g) cooking apples
1 lb (½ kg) castor sugar
12 oz (300 g) butter
4 eggs
1¼ lb (500 g) plain flour
3 level teaspoons baking powder
2 level teaspoons mixed spice

1. Place sultanas and cider in a basin, then cover with a plate and leave in a cool place overnight.
2. Prepare a moderate oven (350°F, 180°C, Gas Mark 4). Brush a large 5 pint capacity (12 in by 10 in) roasting tin with a little melted fat. Line the base with greaseproof paper, then grease paper.
3. Peel and core apples; weigh 1 lb (400 g) of prepared apples and chop finely.
4. Cream the sugar and butter together in a bowl until light and fluffy. Beat the eggs and add them gradually, beating well after each addition.
5. Sift the flour, baking powder and mixed spice together on to a plate; add to the creamed mixture with the chopped apples, sultanas and any remaining cider. Mix well with a metal spoon. Turn mixture into prepared tin; level the top.
6. Bake in centre of oven for 1½ to 1¾ hours. Test by pressing with the fingers. If cooked, cake should spring back and have begun to shrink from sides of tin. Leave to cool in tin; turn out and remove paper.

MEN AND WOMEN AT WORK

Monday

☆ Pickled corned beef sandwiches

Fruit pie

Tuesday

☆ Caponata Crumble Flan

Tomato and onion salad

Lemon mousse

Wednesday

★ Scotch Egg Roll

☆ Pineapple coleslaw

Fruit cake

Thursday

☆ Sausage relish rolls

Cheese straws

★ Dairy Yogurt Dessert

Friday

Cheese and onion flan

Mushroom and celery salad

Wholemeal roll and butter

Fresh fruit

★ see recipe opposite
☆ see daily notes

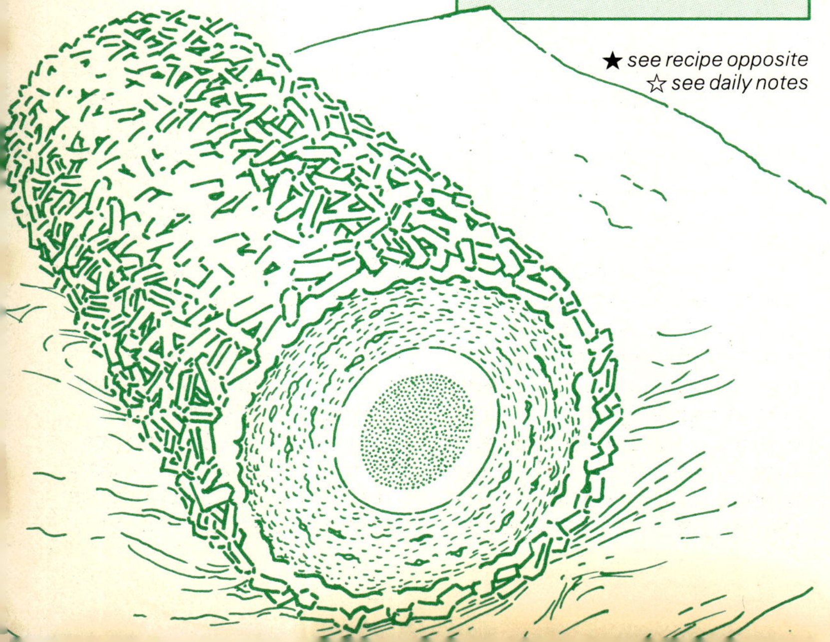

Scotch Egg Roll

Monday

Fill sandwiches with slices of corned beef, spread with a favourite pickle or relish. Serve leftover Sunday pud, or a bought individual fruit pie. **Pack:** spoon. **For tomorrow:** make Caponata Crumble Flan, see page 77. Make or buy lemon mousse.

Tuesday

Slice tomatoes and spring onions and add mayonnaise or salad dressing. **Pack:** knife, fork and spoon. **For tomorrow:** make Scotch Egg Roll. Make or buy coleslaw. Buy a can of pineapple cubes or pieces. Make or buy fruit cake.

Wednesday

Add chopped chunks of pineapple to the coleslaw. **Pack:** knife and fork. **For tomorrow:** grill sausages for roll filling. Make or buy cheese straws. Make Dairy Yogurt Dessert.

Thursday

Fill rolls with sliced cooked sausages and spread with a favourite relish. **Pack:** spoon. **For tomorrow:** make or buy cheese and onion flan. Wash, peel and slice raw mushrooms and celery, store in the fridge.

Friday

Add mayonnaise or salad dressing to the mushrooms and celery. **Pack:** knife and fork.

Scotch Egg Roll

This is economical and, wrapped in cling film, it will keep in the fridge for up to a week.

For 8 portions

Sauce:

1 oz (25 g) margarine
1 oz (25 g) plain flour
¼ pint (5 fl oz) milk
Salt and pepper
¼ level teaspoon dried sage

Filling:

4 eggs
1¼ lb (550 g) thick end belly of pork or pie veal
¾ lb (350 g) pork sausagemeat

Topping:

3 oz (75 g) full fat soft (cream) cheese
3 oz (75 g) butter or margarine
1 small packet potato sticks
1 medium-sized tomato

1. Place the sauce ingredients in a medium-sized saucepan over a low heat; whisk or stir continuously until sauce boils. Cook for 2 minutes, stirring occasionally. Place 1 egg in a bowl and beat, gradually beat into the sauce; leave to cool.
2. Prepare a moderately hot oven (375°F, 180°C, Gas Mark 5). Place a 12 in square of foil on a baking sheet and sprinkle with flour.
3. Hard boil 3 eggs for 10 minutes. Crack and leave to cool in cold water; remove the shells.
4. Remove the bone and skin from pork or veal. Mince or chop meat; stir into sauce.
5. Roll out the sausagemeat to a 10 in by 8 in oblong on floured foil. Spread pork mixture over and arrange eggs down centre.
6. Lift the foil at each side and form into a firm roll; wrap securely at top and ends. Bake in centre of oven for 1¼ hours.
7. Loosen foil at top to allow steam to escape; leave until completely cold.
8. Beat the cream cheese and butter or margarine together; crush potato sticks lightly.
9. Spread cheese mixture over the meat roll, then roll it in crushed potato sticks to coat.

Dairy Yogurt Dessert

This dessert will keep fresh up to a week in the fridge.

For 6 portions

2 level tablespoons or 2 (½ oz) envelopes gelatine
¾ lb (350 g) full fat, soft cream cheese
4 oz (100 g) castor sugar
1 (5.3 oz, 150 g) carton natural yogurt
1 (5.3 oz, 150 g) carton raspberry yogurt
¼ pint (5 fl oz) milk
Knob of butter
6 cookie biscuits, crushed

1. Place 6 tablespoons of water into a small basin; sprinkle over gelatine. Place basin over a pan of hot water. Stir until gelatine has dissolved. Remove from heat.
2. Place the soft cheese and sugar in a bowl; beat until smooth. Place half the mixture in another bowl; whisk the natural yogurt into one bowl and the flavoured yogurt into the other. Whisk half milk and gelatine into each bowl. Leave three minutes, then whisk each again until they thicken.
3. Place tablespoons of the mixture into mould(s), alternating the colours. Smooth top.
4. Melt butter in a saucepan; stir in the biscuits until evenly coated. Press biscuits on top of yogurt mixture. Leave to set.

SCHOOL CHILDREN

Monday

☆ Yeasty egg sandwiches

Cheese-filled celery sticks

Fruit yogurt

Tuesday

★ Caerphilly Salad

Crusty French bread and butter

Chocolate mousse

Wednesday

☆ Baked Chicken Roll

☆ Creamy vegetable salad

Jam tarts

Thursday

Sausage and relish rolls

Orange segment salad

Sponge fingers

Peanuts

Friday

★ Cheesy Apple Pasties

Tomato and potato salad

Fruit cake

Grapes

★ see recipe opposite
☆ see daily notes

Cheesy Apple Pasties

Monday

Yeasty egg sandwiches: mash hard-boiled egg with yeast extract. Grate the cheese to fill the celery sticks. **Pack:** spoon. **For tomorrow:** prepare Caerphilly Salad. Make or buy chocolate mousse.

Tuesday

Pack: fork and spoon. **For tomorrow:** make Baked Chicken Roll, see page 63. Have spare cooked vegetables – peas, carrots, potatoes etc, for creamy vegetable salad. Make or buy jam tarts.

Wednesday

Add mayonnaise to cooked chopped vegetables. **Pack:** knife and fork. **For tomorrow:** grill sausages. Peel and segment orange and sprinkle with soft brown sugar.

Thursday

Spread rolls with favourite relish, lay sliced cooked sausage on top. **Pack:** spoon. **For tomorrow:** make Cheesy Apple Pasties. Cook potatoes for salad. Make or buy fruit cake.

Friday

Add sliced tomatoes and mayonnaise to salad and sprinkle with chopped parsley. **Pack:** knife and fork.

Caerphilly Salad

Mild, moist, textured Caerphilly cheese combined with crunchy celery and sweet grapes makes a delicious and nutritious salad.

Serves 2

4 sticks celery
4 oz (100 g) black grapes
6 oz (175 g) Caerphilly cheese
4 level tablespoons thick mild mayonnaise
Salt and pepper

1. Thoroughly wash celery. Cut into small pieces. Wash the grapes; dry on kitchen paper. Halve the grapes; remove pips.
2. Cut the cheese into small cubes. Place in a bowl with the celery and grapes. Add mayonnaise and salt and pepper. Mix well. Divide between two plastic containers and store in the fridge.

Cheesy Apple Pasties

Ideal for packed meals, these pasties can be served hot with vegetables for supper.

Makes 4 pasties

Pastry:
8 oz (200 g) plain flour
½ level teaspoon salt
2 oz (50 g) margarine
2 oz (50 g) lard

Filling:
1 medium-sized cooking apple
1 stick celery
6 oz (175 g) Leicester cheese
1 level teaspoon made English mustard
Salt and pepper
Beaten egg or milk, to glaze

1. Prepare a moderately hot oven (400°F, 200°C, Gas Mark 6).
2. Place the flour and salt in a bowl, add fats, cut into small pieces, and rub in until mixture resembles fine breadcrumbs. Add about 2 tablespoons of cold water and mix with a fork to form a firm dough. Turn out on to a lightly-floured surface and knead lightly. Wrap in cling film and place in the fridge while preparing filling.
3. Peel and core the apple. Grate coarsely into a bowl. Wash the celery and chop; add to the apple. Cut cheese into ½ in cubes; add to bowl with mustard, 1 level teaspoon salt, and a good shake of pepper. Mix well.
4. Divide pastry into four. Roll each piece to a circle about 6 in across. Trim edges by cutting round a 6 in saucer with a sharp knife.
5. Divide the filling between the circles, placing it in a line across the centre to within ½ in of edges. Dampen edges, press together to seal. Pinch join between fingers and thumb to form fluted edge.
6. Place pasties on a baking sheet, fluted edge uppermost. Brush with beaten egg or milk. Bake in the centre of the oven for 20 to 25 minutes until golden brown.

SCHOOL CHILDREN

Monday

☆ Cheese and pineapple chunks

Sausage rolls

Fresh fruit salad

Tuesday

☆ Crispy Beef Triangles

Tomato and cress salad

Peanuts

Chocolate bar

Wednesday

☆ Cheesy ham twists

Wholemeal roll and butter

★ Nutty Apple Cake

Thursday

☆ Savoury peanut butter sandwiches

Hard-boiled egg

Stewed apple

Sponge fingers

Friday

★ Potted Pilchard Spread rolls

☆ Three Cs salad

Cup cake

Nuts and sultanas

★ see recipe opposite
☆ see daily notes

Potted Pilchard Spread

Monday

Cut cubes of cheese, spear on toothpicks with cubes of canned pineapple. Sprinkle fresh fruit salad with sugar if necessary. **Pack:** spoon. **For tomorrow:** make Crispy Beef Triangles, see page 65.

Tuesday

Add salad cream or French dressing to the salad. **Pack:** knife and fork. **For tomorrow:** Prepare cheesy ham twists. Make Nutty Apple Cake.

Wednesday

Spread cream cheese on a slice of ham, roll up ham and secure with a toothpick. **Pack:** knife and fork. **For tomorrow:** grate cheese. Hard boil egg. Stew apple.

Thursday

Add grated cheese and sliced tomato to the peanut butter for the filling. Halve and season hard-boiled egg. **Pack:** spoon. **For tomorrow:** make Potted Pilchard Spread. Prepare Three Cs salad: chop celery, grate raw carrot, and add cress.

Friday

Spread buttered rolls with Potted Pilchard Spread. Add mayonnaise to the salad. **Pack:** fork.

Nutty Apple Cake

Add apple for an economical and moist fruit cake. It will keep well for up to a week, wrapped in foil or in a cake tin, but not an air-tight container.

1 large cooking apple
1 oz (25 g) walnuts
6 oz (150 g) castor sugar
6 oz (150 g) soft margarine
8 oz (200 g) self-raising flour
1 rounded teaspoon mixed spice
3 eggs
1 tablespoon milk
1 oz (25 g) demerara sugar

1. Prepare a cool oven (325°F, 160°C, Gas Mark 3). Grease a round 7 in cake tin. Line the base with greaseproof paper; grease the paper.
2. Peel and core the apple. Cut 6 thin slices and place in a bowl of cold water. Chop remainder. Roughly chop the walnuts.
3. Place the sugar, margarine, flour, mixed spice, eggs and milk into a mixing bowl. Mix together with a wooden spoon, then beat for 2 to 3 minutes (or 1 to 2 minutes if using an electric mixer) until mixture is smooth and glossy.
4. Fold chopped apple and walnuts into the cake mixture with a metal spoon. Place mixture in prepared tin, levelling top with the back of a metal spoon Drain reserved apple slices and arrange in a ring around top of cake. Sprinkle top with demerara sugar.
5. Bake in centre of oven for 1 hour 20 minutes to 1 hour 30 minutes. Test by pressing with the fingers; if cooked, the cake will spring back and have begun to shrink from sides of tin. Leave to cool in the tin for 15 minutes, turn out on to a wire rack and leave until cold.

Potted Pilchard Spread

This can be stored in the fridge for up to three days. To freeze, cover the dish or pots with foil.

For 8 portions

1 large (15 oz, 425 g) can pilchards in tomato sauce
½ small lemon
Sauce:
2½ oz (65 g) margarine
2½ oz (65 g) plain flour
½ pint (10 fl oz) milk
Salt and pepper

1. Empty contents of the can of pilchards into a bowl. Remove skin and bones; mash pilchards with a fork.
2. Squeeze juice from lemon.
3. Melt margarine in a medium-sized saucepan. Stir in the flour; cook gently, without browning for 2 minutes. Add milk; bring to boil, stirring continuously. Cook for 2 minutes. Taste and season.
4. Remove sauce from heat; stir in the pilchards and 1 tablespoon lemon juice. Mix well. Place mixture in a ½ pint dish or 8 individual pots; smooth top and leave until cold.

SCHOOL CHILDREN

Monday

☆ Salami and celery double decker

Apple and pear yogurt

Sponge fingers

Tuesday

☆ Creamy stuffed eggs

Mini pork sausages

Crispy roll and butter

Blackberry and apple pie

Wednesday

★ Sausage and Apple Puff

Cheese filled celery sticks

Crisps

Grape and orange salad

Thursday

☆ Cream cheese and sultana roll-ups

Apple and banana

Treacle tart

★ see recipe opposite
☆ see daily notes

Friday

★ Cheesy Peanut Crisps

☆ Rosy cheese and relish

Lemon mousse

Mini chocolate roll

Sausage and Apple Puff

Monday

See page 41 for how to make double decker sandwiches. Use salami slices for one layer, salad cream and chopped celery for the other. **Pack:** spoon. **For tomorrow:** hard boil eggs, cool, slice lengthwise; mix yolks with grated cheese and seasoning and re-pack in egg whites. Grill sausages. Make or buy fruit pie.

Tuesday

Pack stuffed eggs on a paper or plastic plate covered with cling film. **Pack:** spoon. **For tomorrow:** make Sausage and Apple Puff. Grate cheese. Prepare grapes and oranges for salad.

Wednesday

Fill celery sticks with grated cheese. **Pack:** knife, fork and spoon. **For tomorrow:** make or buy treacle tart.

Thursday

Mix the cream cheese with a few sultanas and see page 43 for how to make roll-ups. **Pack:** fork (if it's a piece of a large treacle tart). **For tomorrow:** make Cheesy Peanut Crisps. Buy some Edam cheese. Make or buy mousse.

Friday

Cut slices of Edam cheese, each with a piece of rosy red rind on it, lay a slice on each Cheesy Peanut Crisp. Pack relish, or pickle, in a well-sealed container, for spreading on the cheese. **Pack:** knife and spoon.

Sausage and Apple Puff

This can be kept whole or cut into pieces, wrapped in foil or cling film and kept in the fridge for up to a week. Or pack for the freezer and store up to two months.

For 4 to 6 portions

Filling:

1 large onion
1 oz (25 g) margarine
1 large cooking apple
¾ lb (350 g) sausagemeat
1 level teaspoon salt
Pepper

Pastry:

1 large (14 oz, 397 g) packet frozen puff pastry, thawed
Beaten egg or milk to glaze

1. Prepare a moderately hot oven (400°F, 200°C, Gas Mark 6).
2. Peel and chop the onion. Melt margarine in a medium-sized saucepan, add onion and cook gently for 5 minutes, without browning.
3. Peel, core and chop the apple. Add to the saucepan and continue cooking for a further 5 minutes.
4. Remove from heat and stir in the sausagemeat, the salt and a shake of pepper.
5. Divide the pastry into two. Roll out one piece to line an 8 in pie plate. Roll out remaining pastry to a 10 in by 11 in oblong; using a 2½ in plain cutter, cut out 14 rounds.
6. Spread filling over the pastry in the pie plate and level top with the back of a metal spoon. Brush pastry edge with water. Place pastry circles around edge of dish, overlapping, covering pastry edge. Press edges together gently. Brush circles with beaten egg or milk.
7. Place pie on a baking sheet. Bake just above centre of oven for 35 to 40 minutes until pastry is golden brown.

Cheesy Peanut Crisps

These savoury biscuits are cheap to make and they store well in an airtight tin, or the uncooked roll will keep for a week in the fridge, or two months in the freezer.

Makes about 25 biscuits

4 oz (100 g) Leicester cheese
8 oz (200 g) plain flour
2 level teaspoons salt
1 level teaspoon dry mustard
4 oz (100 g) margarine
3 level tablespoons peanut butter
1 egg
2 tablespoons milk
Celery seeds, optional

1. Finely grate the cheese. Place flour, salt and mustard in a bowl. Add margarine, cut into small pieces, and rub in until mixture resembles fine breadcrumbs.
2. Add the cheese and mix with a knife until evenly distributed. Add peanut butter, egg and milk and mix to form a soft dough. Turn out on to a floured surface; knead lightly.
3. Form the mixture into a roll about 2½ in across; wrap in cling film or foil; chill for 2 hours.
4. To cook: prepare a moderately hot oven (375°F, 190°C, Gas Mark 5). Lightly grease a baking sheet. Using a sharp knife, slice the roll thinly. Place the biscuits on a baking sheet and sprinkle with celery seeds, if desired. Bake for 10 to 12 minutes until pale golden at the edges. Cool on a wire rack.

SCHOOL CHILDREN

Monday

☆ Sausage and cheese kebabs

Wholemeal roll and butter

Fruit pie

Tuesday

★ Caponata Crumble Flan

Hazelnut yogurt

Chocolate bar

Wednesday

☆ Scotch Egg Roll

Cheese straws

Apple and blackberry stew

Thursday

☆ Cheesy veg sandwiches

Peanuts

Jam tarts

Friday

Fish pâté and tomato rolls

Potato sticks

★ Banana Mallow Pie

★ see recipe opposite
☆ see daily notes

Caponata Crumble Flan

Monday

Spear slices of cooked sausages and cubes of hard cheese on to toothpicks to make the kebabs. Serve up Sunday's leftover pud or a bought individual fruit pie. **Pack:** spoon. **For tomorrow:** make Caponata Crumble Flan.

Tuesday

If the consumer doesn't care for hazelnut yogurt, supply another fruity flavour that's popular. **Pack:** knife, fork and spoon. **For tomorrow:** make Scotch Egg Roll, see page 69. Make or buy cheese straws. Stew apples and blackberries.

Wednesday

Pack the stewed apples and blackberries in a well-sealed container to avoid leakages. **Pack:** knife, fork and spoon. **For tomorrow:** grate cheese and raw carrot and mix together for sandwiches: add a few sultanas if liked. Make or buy jam tarts.

Thursday

Make up the cheesy veg sandwiches. **Pack:** nothing, all this little lot can be finger eaten. **For tomorrow:** buy or make fish pâté, or use canned fish filling, or fish paste. Buy potato sticks or another savoury-type biscuits. Make Banana Mallow Pie.

Friday

Fill rolls with fish pâté and sliced tomato. **Pack:** fork.

Caponata Crumble Flan

This is delicious hot, too.

For 4 portions

Pastry:
6 oz (170 g) plain flour
½ level teaspoon salt
1½ oz (45 g) margarine
1½ oz (40 g) lard

Filling:
1 small onion
Salt and pepper
1 small green pepper
1 small red pepper
Half a small cucumber
1 medium-sized tomato
2 tablespoons oil

Topping:
1 egg
3 tablespoons milk
2 oz (50 g) fresh white breadcrumbs
1 oz (25 g) shredded suet
1 tablespoon chopped parsley
Salt and pepper

1. Prepare a moderately hot oven (400°F, 200°C, Gas Mark 6). Place an 8 in flan ring on a baking sheet. Place flour and salt in a bowl. Add fats and rub in until mixture resembles fine breadcrumbs.
2. Add about 1½ tablespoons cold water and mix with a fork to form a firm dough. Turn out on to a floured board and knead. Roll out and line the flan ring.
3. Bake flan case blind in centre of oven for 15 minutes; remove paper, beans and flan ring. Return to oven and cook for 5 more minutes.
4. Peel and thinly slice onion.
5. Cut peppers in halves lengthwise; remove seeds, core and white pith. Cut peppers into thin strips lengthwise. Wash and slice cucumber. Skin and roughly chop tomato. Heat oil in a medium-sized saucepan. Add onion and tomato, cover and cook over a moderate heat, stirring occasionally, for 10 minutes.
6. Add the peppers and cucumber; continue cooking uncovered, stirring occasionally, for 10 minutes; taste, season.
7. Spread vegetables over base of flan. Beat egg and milk together in a bowl and pour over vegetables. Place breadcrumbs, suet, parsley, ½ level teaspoon salt and pepper in a basin, mix, sprinkle over flan.
8. Return flan to oven and cook for a further 10 minutes.

Banana Mallow Pie

When cold, wrap individual portions in foil.

For 4 to 6 portions

1 8 in baked, cooled flan case

Filling:
3 bananas
2 lemons
½ pint, (10 fl oz) sweetened condensed milk

Glaze:
1 level dessertspoon redcurrant jelly

1. To make filling: peel and slice 1½ bananas; arrange in base of cooled flan case.
2. Scrub the lemons; grate rind finely from one lemon and squeeze juice from both. Place in a basin. Add condensed milk; stir until mixture thickens. Pour over bananas in flan case.
3. Peel and slice remaining 1½ bananas; arrange slices, overlapping, over lemon filling.
4. To make glaze: place the redcurrant jelly and 1 tablespoon water in a small saucepan; heat slowly, stirring, until jelly melts. Bring to boil, when bubbling quickly, brush over banana.

Monday

Paprika chicken drumstick

Cucumber and raw carrot cubes

Natural yogurt

Apple

Tuesday

Low-calorie soup

★ Country Cottage Dip

Celery

Melon

Wednesday

★ Savoury Shrimp Salad

Grapes

Thursday

Consommé

★ Danish Stuffed Eggs

★ Minted Orange and Grapefruit

★ *see recipes opposite*

Note: all (except Friday) accompanied by crispbread spread thinly with poly-unsaturated fat.

Friday

Ham and lettuce wheatgerm roll

Tomato

Fresh fruit salad

Minted Orange and Grapefruit

Monday

Either save a drumstick from the week-end chicken or cook one with other meals in the oven over the week-end, sprinkle with paprika. Cube the cucumber and grate some raw carrot. **Pack:** fork and spoon, crispbread. **For tomorrow:** prepare the Country Cottage Dip and celery sticks.

Tuesday

Heat the soup and pour into a vacuum flask. Slice or cube the melon for easy eating and put in a container. **Pack:** spoon, crispbread. **For tomorrow:** prepare the Savoury Shrimp Salad.

Wednesday

Pack: fork, crispbread. **For tomorrow:** make or buy consommé. Prepare the Danish Stuffed Eggs and Minted Orange and Grapefruit.

Thursday

Pour the heated consommé in a vacuum flask. **Pack:** knife, fork, spoon and crispbread. **For tomorrow:** make up a fresh fruit salad from any fruit left over from the week. Put in a sealed container with a little lemon juice and keep overnight in the fridge.

Friday

Fill wheatgerm roll with ham and lettuce. Cut up tomato and sprinkle with salt if wished. **Pack:** fork and spoon.

Country Cottage Dip

Eat this dip with celery sticks.

4 oz (100 g) cottage cheese
1 (5.3 oz, 150 g) carton natural low-fat yogurt
1 medium-sized carrot

Mix the cottage cheese and yogurt in a basin. Peel the carrot and grate finely into the cheese mixture; mix together.

Savoury Shrimp Salad

You can garnish this salad with cucumber wedges and tomato slices.

For 2 portions

1 medium-sized carrot
1 stick of celery
¼ medium-sized green pepper
½ teaspoon lemon juice
2 level tablespoons low-calorie vinegar and oil dressing
Salt and pepper
7 oz (200 g) canned or de-frosted shrimps
Lettuce leaves, shredded

1. Peel the carrot and wash the celery. Cut the carrot, celery and pepper into small dice. Place in a bowl with lemon juice, vinegar and oil dressing and seasoning.
2. Drain the shrimps, if you're using canned ones; add to the bowl and stir lightly.
3. Place the shredded lettuce in a plastic container with a lid and top with the shrimp mixture.

Danish Stuffed Eggs

To transport, place on a paper or plastic plate and cover with cling film. Danish Blue cheese gives a tangy flavour.

For 2 portions

2 eggs
Knob of Danish Blue cheese
Salt and pepper
1½ level tablespoons low-calorie vinegar and oil dressing

1. Hard boil the eggs for 10 minutes. Crack and leave to cool in cold water, then shell. Cut in halves lengthwise and scoop out the yolks.
2. Place the yolks in a basin with the cheese and seasoning. Beat well with a wooden spoon until smooth.
3. Beat in the low-calorie vinegar and oil dressing. Place the mixture in the egg halves.

Minted Orange and Grapefruit

Wrap the filled grapefruit shells in cling film. This keeps well in the fridge.

For 4 portions

2 grapefruit
1 large orange
2 rounded teaspoons chopped mint

1. Cut each grapefruit in half; cut around the fruit segments with a sharp, pointed knife. Place the fruit in a basin; reserve the grapefruit shells.
2. Using a sharp knife, cut the peel and pith from the orange. Holding the orange over a basin to catch the juice, cut out segments. Place the segments in a basin with the grapefruit. Add the chopped mint and mix. Leave in a cool place for at least 1 hour for the flavours to blend.
3. Place the mixture into the grapefruit shells.

Monday

Low-calorie soup

☆ Ham surprise salad

Endive

Tuesday

★ Country Potted Tuna

☆ Raw cauliflower and mushroom salad

Lettuce

Stewed plums

Wednesday

☆ Minty chicken drumstick

Carrot, sultana and shredded cabbage salad

Edam cheese

Thursday

★ Sweet and Savoury Spread

Pear and apple salad

★ see recipes opposite
☆ see daily notes
Note: all accompanied by crispbread spread thinly with poly-unsaturated fat.

Friday

Cold lean pork chop

Coleslaw

Tomatoes

Apple purée

Sweet and Savoury Spread

Monday

Heat soup, pour into vacuum flask. For the salad, mix chopped ham, cottage cheese and halved, stoned, black grapes. Prepare endive. **Pack:** fork, crispbread. **For tomorrow:** prepare the Country Potted Tuna. For the salad, cut florets from raw cauliflower, wash. Prepare and slice the raw mushroom, mix together. Wash lettuce. Stew plums.

Tuesday

Pack: knife for spreading tuna, fork and spoon, crispbread. **For tomorrow:** cook chicken drumstick and sprinkle with chopped mint. Prepare salad on a plate, cover with cling film. Cube the Edam cheese.

Wednesday

Pack: fork, crispbread. **For tomorrow:** make the Sweet and Savoury Spread and cut up the pear and apple salad covering with a little lemon juice to stop browning.

Thursday

Pack: a few slices of crispbread with a knife for the spread, spoon. **For tomorrow:** cook a pork chop when you have the oven on. Buy a carton of coleslaw or make some with the cabbage from Wednesday. Make the apple purée.

Friday

Quarter the tomatoes or take whole if wished. **Pack:** knife, fork and spoon, crispbread.

Country Potted Tuna

This can be cut into individual portions and stored in the freezer. Or non-slimmers would enjoy it spread on toast.

For 8 portions

½ lb (225 g) cod fillet
1 small onion
Half a medium-sized lemon
½ level teaspoon salt
Pepper
2 level teaspoons cornflour
¼ level teaspoon dry mustard
¼ level teaspoon cayenne pepper
1 large (7 oz, 198 g) can tuna
Glaze:
1 level teaspoon gelatine
½ teaspoon Worcester sauce

1. Remove skin from the fish. Peel and finely chop the onion. Cut 2 slices from the lemon and reserve; squeeze juice from the remainder. Place in a medium-sized saucepan, with fish, onion, salt, a shake of pepper and ¼ pint (5 fl oz) water.
2. Bring to boil. Cover and simmer for 6 to 7 minutes. Remove fish from the pan, using a draining spoon. Reserve liquor in the pan. Place the fish in a bowl; flake with a fork. Remove any bones and leave to cool.
3. Blend the cornflour, mustard and cayenne pepper with a little of the reserved liquor. Stir into the liquor in the pan. Bring to boil, stirring continuously, and cook for 1 minute. Leave to cool.
4. Drain the liquor from can of tuna. Mix sauce and tuna into flaked fish with a fork. Press into a shallow, 1 pint serving dish. Level top and chill in the fridge.
5. For the glaze: measure 3 tablespoons cold water into a small basin; add gelatine. Place the basin in a saucepan of water over a moderate heat; stir until gelatine has dissolved. Remove basin from heat and stir in Worcester sauce. Leave until cool, but not set.
6. Cut reserved lemon slices into quarters and arrange on top of the fish mixture. Pour gelatine over the surface; chill, until set.

Sweet and Savoury Spread

This will store for a few days in the fridge.

For 2 to 3 portions

1 small cooking apple
2 or 3 spring onions
6 oz (175 g) cooked lean meat
1 tablespoon Worcester sauce
1 level dessertspoon low-calorie salad dressing
1 level teaspoon made mustard
Seasoning

1. Peel and core the apple and roughly chop. Trim and wash the onions; roughly chop with the meat. Mince the apple, onions and meat together.
2. Add the remaining ingredients and mix well. Place the mixture in a suitable container, cover with foil.

MEN AND WOMEN AT WORK

Monday

Vegetable soup

Cold meat and pickle rolls

Fresh fruit

Tuesday

★ Mushroom and Cottage Cheese Flan

Vegetable salad

Fruit pie

Wednesday

Liver pâté crispy rolls

☆ Russian-style Potato Salad

Orange mousse

Thursday

☆ Sausages and spicy dip

Finger rolls and butter

★ Tango Cheesecake

Friday

Oxtail soup

☆ Sardine and cress double deckers

☆ Apple Flapjack Squares

★ see recipe opposite
☆ see daily notes

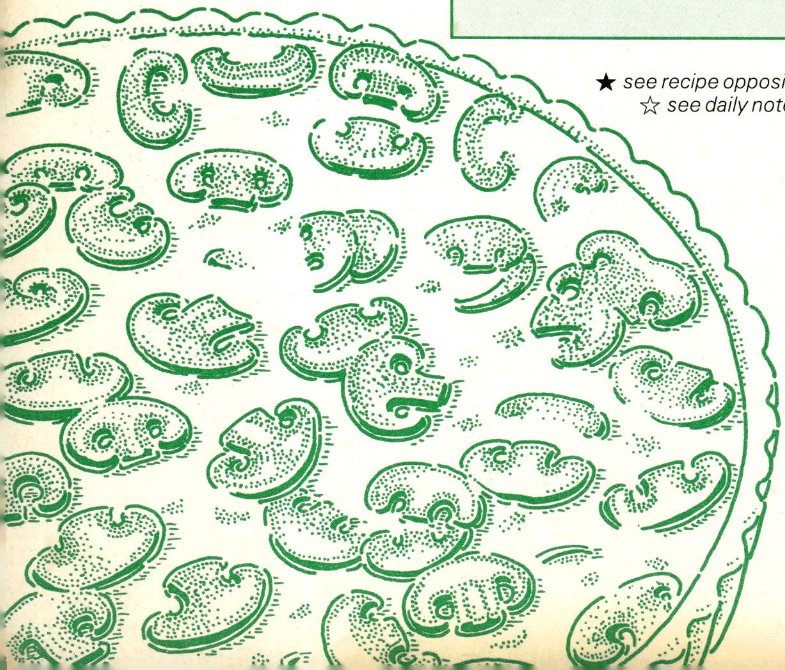

Mushroom and Cottage Cheese Flan

Monday

Pour the heated soup into a vacuum flask. Spread leftover cold meat (or sliced luncheon meat) with a favourite pickle for the rolls. **Pack:** fingers-only menu. **For tomorrow:** make Mushroom and Cottage Cheese Flan. Cook vegetables for salad. Dice when cool and mix with mayonnaise. Make or buy fruit pie.

Tuesday

Pack: knife, fork and spoon. **For tomorrow:** make or buy liver pâté. Make Russian-style Potato Salad, see page 91. Make or buy orange mousse.

Wednesday

Spread crispy rolls with liver pâté, add a few slices of tomato if you have any. **Pack:** fork and spoon. **For tomorrow:** grill sausages. Make Tango Cheesecake.

Thursday

Pack a small container with a favourite relish for the dip. **Pack:** fork. **For tomorrow:** drain a can of sardines and flake the fish. Make double decker sandwiches, see page 41. Use mayonnaise instead of butter on the cress layer if liked. Make Apple Flapjack Squares, see page 91.

Friday

Pour the heated soup into a vacuum flask. **Pack:** fork.

Mushroom and Cottage Cheese Flan

Cut individual portions and wrap in foil, use the remainder for family supper.

For 6 portions

Pastry:

6 oz (150 g) farmhouse or millstone plain flour
¼ level teaspoon salt
4 oz (100 g) margarine

Filling:

1 small (4 oz, 113 g) carton cottage cheese with chives
2 eggs
¼ pint (5 fl oz) milk
1 level teaspoon salt
Pepper
¼ lb (100 g) button mushrooms

1. Prepare a moderate oven (350°F, 180°C, Gas Mark 4). Place an 8½ in fluted flan tin on a baking sheet.
2. Place flour and salt in a bowl. Add the margarine, cut into small pieces and rub in until mixture resembles fine breadcrumbs. Add about 1 tablespoon water and mix with a fork to form a firm dough.
3. Turn out on to a floured board and knead lightly. Roll out to a circle, 1½ in larger all around than flan tin. Line the flan tin.
4. Place the cottage cheese, eggs, milk, salt and shake of pepper in a basin; beat together.
5. Wash, dry and slice the mushrooms, add to basin. Pour mixture into flan.
6. Cook in centre of oven for 30 to 35 minutes, until filling is set.

Tango Cheesecake

Cut into individual portions, wrap and freeze.

For 6 to 8 portions

Base:

4 oz (100 g) digestive biscuits
2 oz (50 g) butter or margarine
2 level tablespoons chocolate spread

Filling:

1 lime or lemon
8 oz (225 g) cottage cheese
¼ pint (5 fl oz) natural yogurt
2 oz (50 g) castor sugar
1 lime-flavoured jelly

1. Butter an 8 in round pie plate. Place the biscuits between two sheets of greaseproof paper and crush finely with a rolling pin
2. Place the butter and chocolate spread in a saucepan. Heat gently until the butter has melted. Remove from heat; stir in the crushed biscuits. Press into pie plate.
3. Slice half of the lime or lemon thinly; reserve. Finely grate the rind and squeeze juice from the other half. Press the cottage cheese through a sieve into a basin. Stir in yogurt, sugar and grated rind and juice; mix well.
4. Place the jelly cubes in a small saucepan with 5 tablespoons water. Heat gently, stirring until jelly has dissolved. Pour into measuring jug and make up to ¾ pint (15 fl oz) with cold water or ice. Leave until almost set.
5. Whisk the jelly until light and foamy. Whisk in the cheese mixture gradually. When just set pile into prepared case.
6. Cut each reserved lime or lemon slice into 4, arrange overlapping around edge of cheesecake. Chill.

MEN AND WOMEN AT WORK

Monday

Mulligatawny soup

Egg mayonnaise baps

Fresh fruit

Tuesday

Bacon and tomato wholemeal rolls

☆ Chocolate Mint Whip

Wednesday

★ Spaghetti Tuna Loaf

Green salad

Lemon mousse

Thursday

☆ Sausage Roulade

Coleslaw

Crusty French bread and butter

Fresh fruit salad

★ *see recipe opposite*
☆ *see daily notes*

Friday

Onion soup

Finger rolls and butter

Cheese, chicory and leek salad

★ Spicy Brew Bread

Spicy Brew Bread

Monday

Pour the heated soup into a vacuum flask. Make egg mayonnaise filling by mashing hard-boiled eggs with mayonnaise and seasoning. **Pack:** fingers-only, unless the consumer wants to peel the fruit. **For tomorrow:** make Chocolate Mint Whip, see page 93.

Tuesday

Slice tomatoes and grill bacon (removing rinds) for roll filling. **Pack:** spoon. **For tomorrow:** make Spaghetti Tuna Loaf. Prepare green salad. Make or buy lemon mousse.

Wednesday

If you're using lettuce in the salad, pack the dressing separately in a well-sealed container. **Pack:** knife, fork and spoon. **For tomorrow:** make Sausage Roulade, see page 93. Make or buy coleslaw. Prepare fresh fruit salad. **NB for Friday:** prepare fruit for Spicy Brew Bread.

Thursday

Pack: knife, fork and spoon. **For tomorrow:** make or buy onion soup. Wash and slice chicory and leeks for salad. Make Spicy Brew Bread.

Friday

Pour the heated soup into a vacuum flask. Cube cheese and add to the salad. **Pack:** fork.

Spaghetti Tuna Loaf

This will keep in the fridge for up to 3 days. Serve remainder for family supper.

For 8 portions

4 oz (100 g) spaghetti
2 oz (50 g) fresh white breadcumbs
2 (7 oz, 198 g) cans tuna
1 small can evaporated milk
1 level teaspoon grated onion
2 teaspoons lemon juice
½ level teaspoon salt
Pepper
3 eggs

1. Break the spaghetti into 1 in lengths. Cook in a large saucepan of boiling salted water for about 10 minutes, or as directed on packet. Drain in a sieve or colander and rinse with cold water. Place in a bowl.
2. Prepare a cool oven (325°F, 170°C, Gas Mark 3). Brush a 2 lb (2½ pint capacity) loaf tin with melted fat. Coat the base and the sides of tin with a thin layer of breadcrumbs, pressing firmly with the fingers.
3. Add the drained tuna to the spaghetti in the bowl. Break up the tuna with a fork into small pieces. Make up the milk to ½ pint (10 fl oz) with water; add to the bowl with the onion, lemon juice, the salt and a shake of pepper.
4. Beat the eggs stir into the mixture in the bowl. Pour into loaf tin; cover top with a piece of foil.
5. Bake in the centre of oven for 50 to 55 minutes, until mixture feels firm and has set. Leave to cool in the tin.
6. Remove foil, invert loaf on to a serving dish; cut pieces and wrap in foil.

Spicy Brew Bread

The loaves will improve in flavour if stored for up to 4 weeks in a tin.

Makes 2 loaves

1 lb (400 g) mixed dried fruit
½ pint (10 fl oz) brown ale
8 oz (200 g) granulated sugar
1 egg
2 rounded tablespoons thick-cut marmalade
8 oz (200 g) plain flour
8 oz (200 g) wheatmeal flour
4 level teaspoons baking powder

1. Place the fruit in a bowl. Add the ale and sugar; mix together. Leave to soak overnight.
2. Prepare a cool oven (325°F, 170°C, Gas Mark 3). Grease 2 (1 lb, 1½ pint capacity) loaf tins.
3. Stir the egg and marmalade into the fruit mixture. Add the flours and baking powder; mix well. Divide the mixture between tins; level the tops with back of spoon.
4. Bake in centre of oven for 1½ hours, until well risen. Test by pressing with the fingers. If cooked, loaves should spring back and have begun to shrink from sides of tins. Leave to cool in the tins for 10 minutes, then turn out and leave to cool completely on a wire rack. Serve sliced and buttered.

Monday

Sausage and ketchup rolls

Vegetable salad

Fresh fruit

Tuesday

★ Potted Bacon Spread

Crusty French bread and butter

Fruit crumble

Wednesday

☆ Wheaty Oatcakes

☆ Three-cheese cubes

Orange and banana salad

Thursday

Irish stew

★ Spiced Citrus Cocktail

★ *see recipe opposite*
☆ *see daily notes*

Friday

Spring vegetable soup

Crunchy chicken drumsticks

Wholemeal roll and butter

☆ Yogurt and Date Cake

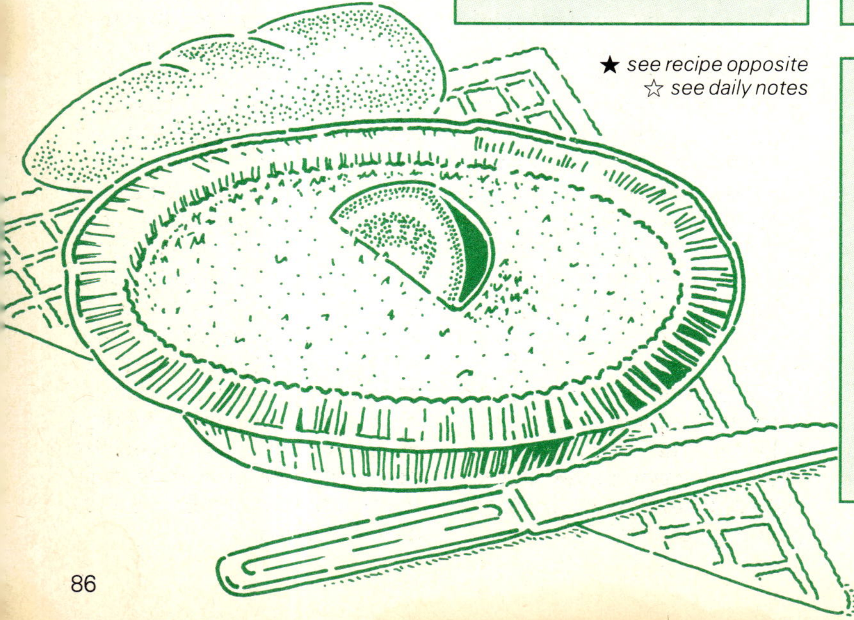

Potted Bacon Spread

Monday

Slice cooked sausages and fill rolls spread with butter and tomato, or other favourite, ketchup. Dice cooked vegetables and add mayonnaise for the salad. **Pack:** fork. **For tomorrow:** make Potted Bacon Spread. Make crumble.

Tuesday

Pack an individual portion of fruit crumble in a well-sealed container. **Pack:** knife and spoon. **For tomorrow:** make Wheaty Oatcakes, see page 95. Buy three different kinds of hardish cheese eg Leicester, Cheddar, Edam. Segment oranges and place in a container.

Wednesday

Take a separate container of butter. Cube the three types of cheese and pack in a container. Peel and slice the banana, sprinkle with lemon juice and add to oranges. **Pack:** knife and spoon. **For tomorrow:** make Irish stew and Spiced Citrus Cocktail.

Thursday

Put heated Irish stew in a wide-necked vacuum flask. **Pack:** knife, fork and spoon. **For tomorrow:** coat chicken drumsticks in wholemeal flour before roasting. Make Yogurt and Date Cake, see page 95.

Friday

Pour heated spring vegetable soup into a vacuum flask. **Pack:** fingers-only menu.

Potted Bacon Spread

This will keep in a fridge for up to 4 days or in a freezer for up to 2 months

For 6 portions

2 lb (1 kg) end piece forehock bacon
1 chicken stock cube
3 peppercorns
¼ level teaspoon ground nutmeg
½ level teaspoon made mustard
2 bay leaves
1 oz (25 g) butter
2 rounded tablespoons thick, mild mayonnaise
2 oz (25 g) fresh white breadcrumbs

1. Remove the rind and excess fat from the bacon. Cut the bacon into 1 in cubes. Place in a medium-sized saucepan. Cover with water, bring to boil and boil rapidly for 5 minutes; drain.
2. Add the stock cube, peppercorns, nutmeg, mustard, bay leaves and 1½ pints (30 fl oz) water to bacon in pan. Bring to boil; cover and simmer for 55 to 60 minutes, until bacon is tender. Strain the meat and reserve stock. Remove peppercorns and bay leaves.
3. Melt the butter in a small saucepan. Place bacon, melted butter, mayonnaise, breadcrumbs and about 9 tablespoons reserved stock in a liquidiser goblet. Run the machine until mixture is well blended. (Alternatively, finely mince the bacon; mix in a basin with other ingredients.)
4. Divide the bacon mixture evenly between 6 individual foil dishes; level top with back of a spoon. Cover with foil.

Spiced Citrus Cocktail

A tangy winter fruit salad. Pack in a well-sealed plastic container for a packed meal.

For 4 portions

4 medium-sized firm oranges
2 small firm grapefruit
Natural demerara sugar
1 cinnamon stick
2 tablespoons orange-flavoured liqueur, optional

1. Scrub 2 oranges. Cut the peel from the oranges taking care not to include pith. Shred the peel thinly and reserve.
2. Cut the peel and white pith from the remaining oranges, grapefruit and pared oranges. Cut fruit into thick slices; discard pips and any thick white pith.
3. Place the shredded peel and ½ pint (10 fl oz) water in a large-based pan, bring to boil and cook 5 minutes. Remove peel and reserve.
4. Add 4 oz (100 g) sugar and the cinnamon stick, broken into four, to the pan; reduce heat and gently add half the fruit slices. Poach the fruit for 4 to 5 minutes. Remove fruit with a draining spoon and place in a warmed dish. Repeat with the remaining fruit.
5. Sprinkle liqueur, if used, over the fruit and pour over the syrup from pan with the cinnamon.
6. Rinse the pan. Place 2 rounded tablespoons sugar and 2 tablespoons water in pan; stir over a low heat until sugar has dissolved. Add the peel, turn up heat and stir continuously until syrup has been absorbed by the peel. Sprinkle peel over fruit. Remove cinnamon sticks before serving.

MEN AND WOMEN AT WORK

Monday

Veal and ham pie

Vegetable salad

Fruit crumble

Tuesday

Oxtail soup

Cheese and onion flan

Wholemeal roll and butter

☆ Brazilian Biscuit Cake

Wednesday

★ Curried Chuna Buns

Coleslaw

Fruit trifle

Thursday

☆ Lemon Chicken Plait

Crusty French bread and butter

Fresh fruit salad

Friday

Chicken and vegetable casserole

★ Chocolate and Cherry Toppers

★ *see recipe opposite*
☆ *see daily notes*

Curried Chuna Buns

Monday

Dice cooked vegetables and mix with mayonnaise for the salad. If you haven't any fruit crumble, pack fresh fruit instead. **Pack:** knife, fork and spoon. **For tomorrow:** make or buy cheese and onion flan. Make Brazilian Biscuit Cake, see page 97.

Tuesday

Pour heated soup into a vacuum flask. **Pack:** fork. **For tomorrow:** make Curried Chuna Buns. Make or buy coleslaw. Make or buy fruit trifle.

Wednesday

Place Curried Chuna Buns in a shallow plastic container with a lid. **Pack:** knife, fork and spoon. **For tomorrow:** make Lemon Chicken Plait, see page 97. Prepare fresh fruit salad.

Thursday

Sprinkle fresh fruit salad with sugar if necessary. **Pack:** knife, fork and spoon. **For tomorrow:** make chicken and vegetable casserole. Make Chocolate and Cherry Toppers.

Friday

Pack the heated chicken and vegetable casserole in a wide-necked vacuum flask. **Pack:** knife and fork.

Curried Chuna Buns

For 6 portions

Choux pastry:

2 oz (50 g) margarine
2½ oz (65 g) plain flour
2 eggs

Filling:

1 oz (25 g) margarine
1 oz (25 g) plain flour
1 level teaspoon curry powder
⅓ pint (6½ fl oz) milk
1 (7 oz, 198 g) can tuna
1 rounded tablespoon thick, mild mayonnaise
1 teaspoon lemon juice
1 rounded teaspoon chopped chives

1. Prepare a moderately hot oven (400°F, 200°C, Gas Mark 6). Brush a baking sheet with melted fat.
2. Place 2 oz (50 g) margarine and ¼ pint (5 fl oz) water in a medium-sized saucepan; bring to boil. Remove from heat and add all the flour immediately; beat well. The mixture should leave sides of pan.
3. Allow to cool slightly. Whisk the eggs and beat into mixture, a little at a time.
4. Place 12 separate spoonfuls of mixture on a baking sheet; bake just above centre of oven for 25 to 30 minutes. Place on a wire rack, split along one side of each to allow steam to escape; leave until cold.
5. To make filling: melt 1 oz margarine in a medium-sized saucepan; stir in flour and curry powder. Cook gently for about 2 minutes, without browning. Add the milk, bring to boil, stirring continuously and cook for 2 minutes. Leave to cool, beating occasionally with a wooden spoon, to prevent a skin.
6. Mash together drained tuna, mayonnaise and lemon juice. Mix in cold sauce and chives.
7. Fill each choux bun with a heaped teaspoonful of mixture.

Chocolate and Cherry Toppers

Keep these, if you can, in a tin.

Makes 18

4 oz (125 g) plain chocolate
4 oz (125 g) glacé cherries
4 oz (125 g) soft margarine
4 oz (125 g) castor sugar
1 egg
8 oz (225 g) plain flour
¼ level teaspoon salt
4 level tablespoons thick honey

1. Prepare a moderate oven (350°F, 180°C, Gas Mark 4).
2. Brush a shallow, 7 in square tin with melted fat. Line base with greased greaseproof.
3. Finely chop half of the chocolate and cherries; coarsely chop remainder and reserve.
4. Cream margarine and sugar together until light and fluffy. Beat egg and add gradually, beating well.
5. Beat in finely-chopped chocolate and cherries. Stir in flour and salt; mix, to form a soft dough.
6. Spread mixture evenly in tin.
7. Bake in centre of oven for 25 to 30 minutes, until biscuit is lightly browned at edges. Leave to cool in tin for 5 minutes; turn out, remove paper and leave to cool on wire rack.
8. Measure honey carefully and place in a saucepan and bring to boil. Stir in reserved chocolate and cherries. Quickly pour topping over biscuit base.
9. When topping has set, cut into 9 squares and cut each square in half.

SCHOOL CHILDREN

Monday

☆ Spicy bacon rolls

Peanuts

Raspberry yogurt

Tuesday

Salami and cream cheese double deckers

Cheese filled celery sticks

Fruit pie

Crisps

Wednesday

Scotch eggs

★ Russian-style Potato Salad

Lemon mousse

Sponge fingers

Thursday

Crunchy chicken drumsticks

Crusty French bread and butter

☆ Tango Cheesecake

Chocolate-covered raisins

★ *see recipe opposite*
☆ *see daily notes*

Friday

Oxtail soup

Tuna fish and celery crispy rolls

★ Apple Flapjack Squares

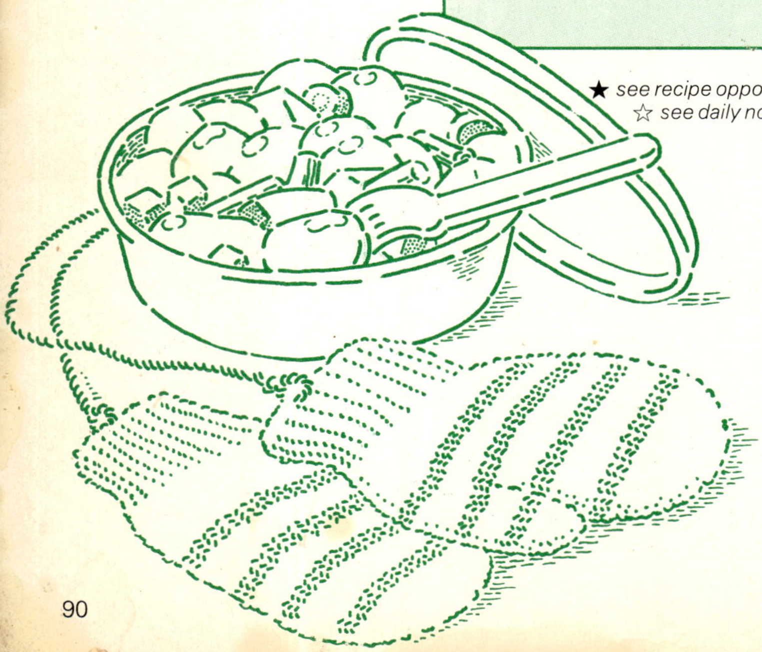

Russian-style Potato Salad

Monday

Grill bacon rashers, remove rind and add, with tomato, or another favourite ketchup to the buttered rolls. **Pack:** spoon. **For tomorrow:** grate cheese for celery sticks. Make or buy fruit pie.

Tuesday

For how to make double decker sandwiches, see page 41. Use salami slices for one layer, cream cheese for the other. **Pack:** fork. **For tomorrow:** make or buy Scotch eggs. Make Russian-style Potato Salad. Make or buy lemon mousse.

Wednesday

Cut Scotch eggs in half for easy eating. **Pack:** fork and spoon. **For tomorrow:** coat chicken drumsticks in wholemeal flour before roasting. Make Tango Cheesecake, see page 83.

Thursday

Wrap chicken drumsticks in foil. **Pack:** fork. **For tomorrow:** drain can of tuna fish and mash with chopped celery for the roll filling. Make Apple Flapjack Squares.

Friday

Pour the heated soup into a vacuum flask. **Pack:** fork.

Russian-style Potato Salad

Covered with foil or cling film, this salad may be stored in the fridge for up to 1 week.

For 3 to 4 portions

1½ lb (¾ kg) potatoes
4 oz (100 g) frozen mixed vegetables
1 small onion
4 rounded tablespoons thick, mild mayonnaise
½ level teaspoon salt
Pepper

1. Scrub and peel the potatoes and cook in boiling, salted water for 20 to 25 minutes. Add the frozen mixed vegetables to the saucepan for last 8 minutes. Drain; allow to cool.
2. Cut the potatoes into large dice. Peel and chop the onion. Place the mayonnaise in a bowl; add vegetables, salt and a shake of pepper. Stir carefully until vegetables are evenly coated with mayonnaise. Place in a serving bowl or individual containers and chill until ready to serve.

Apple Flapjack Squares

Tangy apple purée makes a moist filling for flapjack. It freezes well and can be warmed to serve for pudding.

Makes 15 squares

Filling:
1 lb (½ kg) cooking apples
2 oz (50 g) butter
4 oz (100 g) granulated sugar
2 oz (50 g) seedless raisins

Flapjack:
8 level tablespoons golden syrup
6 oz (175 g) margarine
6 oz (175 g) moist light brown sugar
1 lb (½ kg) rolled (porridge) oats

1. Prepare a moderate oven (350°F, 180°C, Gas Mark 4). Grease a 10 in by 6½ in by 1½ in baking tin.
2. Peel, core and slice the apples. Melt the butter in a saucepan and add apple. Stir over a medium heat for about 10 minutes until apples are pulpy. Remove from heat and beat with a wooden spoon. Add sugar and stir until dissolved. Return to heat and cook over a medium heat for about 10 minutes until mixture is thick enough to leave a mark when the wooden spoon is drawn across the surface. Add raisins and leave to cool.
3. To make flapjack: measure golden syrup carefully; place in a saucepan and add margarine. Leave over a low heat until margarine has melted. Stir in sugar and rolled oats.
4. Spread half the flapjack mixture in tin, pressing mixture down firmly with the back of a metal spoon. Spread the apple filling over the top. Take a tablespoon of remaining flapjack mixture, press with the back of another tablespoon and place on apple. Repeat with remaining mixture, then lightly smooth surface with the back of a wetted tablespoon. Bake in centre of oven for 40 to 50 minutes until firm and golden brown. Leave to cool in the tin, then cut flapjack into 15 squares.

SCHOOL CHILDREN

Monday

☆ Cheesy nutty baps

Satsuma, apple

Crisps

Chocolate-covered raisins

Tuesday

Chicken pasty

Egg and cress salad

★ Chocolate Mint Whip

Wednesday

Tomato soup

Crusty French bread and butter

Cheese and pineapple kebabs

Pear yogurt

Thursday

★ Sausage Roulade

Coleslaw

Mini chocolate Swiss roll

Peanuts

Friday

☆ Tuna fish and cress roll-ups

Orange mousse

Digestive biscuits

★ see recipe opposite
☆ see daily notes

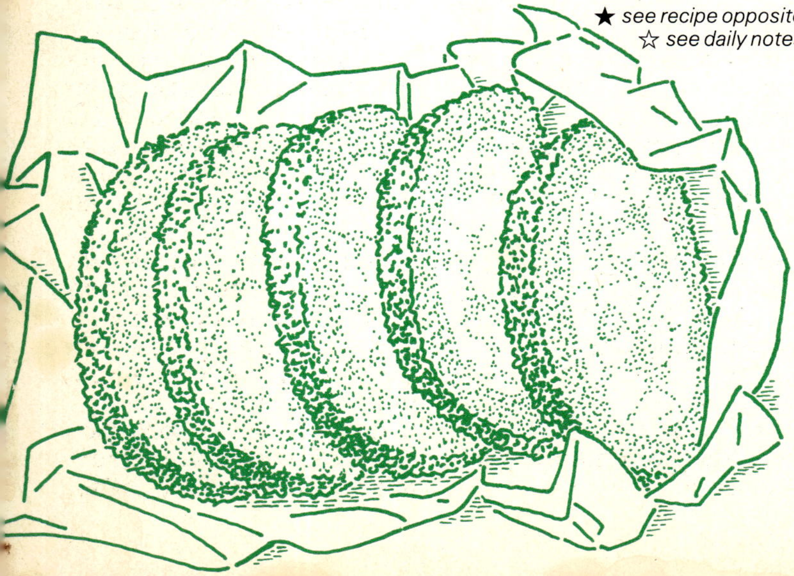

Sausage Roulade

Monday

Spread rolls with peanut butter and then fill with grated cheese. **Pack:** a fingers-only menu. **For tomorrow:** make or buy chicken pasty. Hard boil egg for salad. Make Chocolate Mint Whip.

Tuesday

Pack pasty in foil or cling film and put in a plastic container. Chop hard-boiled egg and add cress and salad cream. **Pack:** knife, fork and spoon. **For tomorrow:** buy a small tin of pineapple cubes and spear a cube of cheese and a pineapple cube on a toothpick for the kebabs.

Wednesday

Pour the heated soup into a vacuum flask. **Pack:** spoon. **For tomorrow:** make Sausage Roulade. Make or buy coleslaw.

Thursday

Pack: knife and fork. **For tomorrow:** drain a tin of tuna fish, flake and mix with cress. See page 43 for how to make roll-ups. Store in the fridge. Make or buy orange mousse.

Friday

Pack: spoon.

Chocolate Mint Whip

Evaporated milk is the base of this rich chocolate dessert. It's cheap to make.

For 4 portions

½ oz (1 envelope) gelatine
4 level tablespoons cocoa
4 level tablespoons castor sugar
1 large can evaporated milk
1 peppermint-flavoured chocolate bar

1. Measure 3 tablespoons of cold water into a large bowl and sprinkle over gelatine; leave to soften.
2. Place the cocoa, sugar and 4 tablespoons cold water in a saucepan. Bring to boil, stirring, and cook 1 minute. Gradually stir in the evaporated milk and bring to boil, stirring. Add to gelatine and mix well.
3. Place bowl in iced water to cool quickly. When cold, chill until almost set.
4. Whisk chocolate mixture until double in volume. Roughly chop the chocolate peppermint bar; stir into the chocolate mixture, reserving a little for decoration.
5. Divide the chocolate mixture between 4 small individual containers, sprinkle each with a little chopped chocolate bar, before packing.

Sausage Roulade

This will keep in a fridge for up to 3 days. Slice thinly to serve.

For 6 to 8 portions

3 eggs
1 large onion
1 oz (25 g) lard
½ lb (225 g) cooked new potatoes
3 oz (75 g) mature Cheddar cheese
½ level teaspoon salt
Pepper
¼ level teaspoon mixed dried herbs
Plain flour
1 lb (½ kg) pork sausagemeat
Browned breadcumbs

1. Prepare a moderate oven (375°F, 190°C, Gas Mark 5). Hard boil 2 eggs for 10 minutes; crack and leave to cool in cold water. Shell and dry on kitchen paper, then cut each egg into 4.
2. Peel and chop the onion. Melt the lard in a medium-sized saucepan; add the onion. Cover and cook over a low heat for about 10 minutes, until tender.
3. Cut potatoes and cheese into ¼ in dice; add to the pan with salt, a shake of pepper and mixed dried herbs. Mix well.
4. Beat remaining egg in a basin; add half to the pan with hard-boiled eggs, mix gently.
5. Sprinkle a large piece of foil with flour and roll out the sausagemeat to an 8 in square on the foil. Pile potato mixture in a line down the centre. Press sausagemeat over filling; join 2 opposite sides, to enclose filling, using foil to lift the sausagemeat. Press filling into ends of roll, wrap tightly in foil and place, joined sides downwards in a roasting tin. Cook in top position of oven for 30 minutes. Remove from oven, open foil, brush sausagemeat with remaining beaten egg and sprinkle with browned breadcrumbs. Return to oven and cook for further 30 minutes, until well browned.
6. Leave in foil to cool, then remove foil and wrap roulade in another piece and keep chilled.

SCHOOL CHILDREN

Monday

☆ Coleslaw-dressed cheesy celery baps

Apple pie

Peanuts

Tuesday

☆ Potted Bacon Spread

Crusty French bread and butter

Pear yogurt

Chocolate biscuits

Wednesday

Tomato soup

★ Wheaty Oatcakes

Cheese slices

Fresh fruit

Thursday

Meat balls and vegetable stew

Orange mousse

Sponge fingers

Friday

Oxtail soup

Wholemeal roll and butter

Scotch egg

★ Yogurt and Date Cake

★ *see recipe opposite*
☆ *see daily notes*

Wheaty Oatcakes

Monday

Mix grated cheese and chopped celery with coleslaw dressing for the baps. You didn't have apple pie for Sunday? Then use a bought one, or fresh fruit. **Pack:** fork. **For tomorrow:** make Potted Bacon Spread, see page 87.

Tuesday

Pack: knife for spreading the Potted Bacon Spread. **For tomorrow:** make or buy tomato soup. Make Wheaty Oatcakes.

Wednesday

Pour the heated soup into a vacuum flask. Pack butter in a well-sealed container. Cut slices of cheese and pack in cling film. **Pack:** knife for butter spreading. **For tomorrow:** make meat balls and vegetable stew. Buy or make mousse.

Thursday

Put the heated stew into a wide-necked vacuum flask. **Pack:** knife, fork and spoon. **For tomorrow:** make or buy Scotch egg. Make Yogurt and Date Cake.

Friday

Pour heated soup into a vacuum flask. Cut Scotch egg in half for easy eating. **Pack:** a fingers-only menu.

Wheaty Oatcakes

Wheatmeal flour and oats give these savoury biscuits a delicious flavour. They will keep fresh in an airtight tin for two weeks, or keep the biscuit dough rolls in the freezer and you will have a constant supply whenever you need them.

Makes about 25 biscuits

4 oz (100 g) wheatmeal flour
4 oz (100 g) medium oatmeal
1 level teaspoon baking powder
1 level teaspoon salt
2 level teaspoons moist brown sugar
4 oz (100 g) butter or margarine
1 tablespoon milk

1. Place the flour, oatmeal, baking powder, salt and sugar in a bowl. Add the fat and rub in until the mixture resembles fine breadcrumbs.
2. Add the milk and mix to form a firm dough. Turn out on to a lightly-floured surface; knead lightly. Form the mixture into a roll about 2 in across; wrap in cling film or foil and chill for at least 2 hours.
3. To cook: prepare moderate oven (350°F, 180°C, Gas Mark 4). Grease a baking sheet. Using a sharp knife, slice the roll thinly. Place biscuits a little apart on a baking sheet and sprinkle with a little oatmeal. Bake for 12 to 15 minutes until light golden. Remove and cool on a wire rack.

Yogurt and Date Cake

This improves in flavour if kept for 2 to 3 days in a tin.

4 oz (125 g) butter
2 oz (50 g) soft dark brown sugar
1 level tablespoon black treacle
3 level tablespoons golden syrup
3 oz (75 g) stoned dates
3 oz (75 g) shelled almonds
¼ pint (5 fl oz) natural yogurt
2 eggs
8 oz (200 g) plain flour
1 level teaspoon mixed spice
½ level teaspoon bicarbonate of soda
Icing sugar

1. Prepare a cool oven (300°F, 150°C, Gas Mark 2). Brush a 2-pint plain ring mould with melted fat.
2. Place the butter and brown sugar in a small saucepan. Measure the black treacle and golden syrup carefully; add to saucepan. Stir over a moderate heat until the butter has melted. Remove from heat and allow to cool.
3. Coarsely chop the dates and almonds. Beat the yogurt and eggs together. Sift the flour, spice and bicarbonate of soda into a bowl. Add dates, almonds, melted mixture and yogurt mixture; mix well with a wooden spoon.
4. Pour the mixture into prepared mould and bake in centre of oven for 60 to 70 minutes. Test by pressing with the fingers. If cooked, cake should spring back and have begun to shrink from sides of mould.
5. Allow to cool in mould for 10 minutes. Invert on to a wire rack, remove mould and leave to cool. Dust with icing sugar.

SCHOOL CHILDREN

Monday

Tomato soup

☆ Yeasty egg rolls

Crisps

Fruit pie or fresh fruit

Tuesday

☆ Salami and coleslaw double deckers

Apple

Orange

★ Brazilian Biscuit Cake

Wednesday

Ham and egg flan

Wholemeal roll and butter

Blackcurrant yogurt

Thursday

★ Lemon Chicken Plait

Crusty French bread and butter

Blackberry and apple stew

Friday

Corned beef hash

Vegetable salad

☆ Chocolate and Cherry Toppers

★ see recipe opposite
☆ see daily notes

Brazilian Biscuit Cake

Monday

Pour heated soup into a vacuum flask. Spread rolls with butter and yeast extract and fill with mashed hard-boiled egg mixed with a little salad cream and seasoning. **Pack:** nothing. **For tomorrow:** make or buy coleslaw. Make the Brazilian Biscuit Cake.

Tuesday

Make salami and coleslaw double deckers, see page 41. **Pack:** another fingers-only menu. **For tomorrow:** make or buy ham and egg flan.

Wednesday

Pack a piece of, or an individual, ham and egg flan in foil and put in a plastic container. Butter and sandwich together the wholemeal roll. **Pack:** fork and spoon. **For tomorrow:** make Lemon Chicken Plait. Stew blackberries and apples.

Thursday

Pack a piece of Lemon Chicken Plait in foil. Butter the French bread. **Pack:** fork and spoon. **For tomorrow:** make corned beef hash. For the salad, cook vegetables, peas, carrots, sweetcorn, potato and dice. Make Chocolate and Cherry Toppers, see page 89.

Friday

Pack heated corned beef hash in a wide-necked vacuum flask. Mix diced veg with salad cream and put in a plastic container. **Pack:** fork.

Brazilian Biscuit Cake

This uncooked chocolate cake is quick and simple to make. Store it in the fridge.

3 level tablespoons golden syrup
4 oz (100 g) margarine
6 oz (175 g) unsalted butter
2 3.5 oz, (100 g) bars plain chocolate
6 oz (175 g) glacé cherries, halved
4 oz (100 g) sultanas
3 tablespoons orange juice
3 tablespoons hot water
5 oz (150 g) rich tea biscuits

1. Line a 7 in or 8 in round tin with foil; brush foil with melted margarine.
2. Measure the syrup carefully; place in a saucepan with margarine and butter. Break up the chocolate and add to pan. Melt contents over a low heat.
3. Add the cherries to pan with the sultanas.
4. Place the orange juice and water in a bowl. Break the biscuits into small pieces, and add to bowl; keep turning biscuits over until all liquid has been absorbed. Stir biscuits into pan, then pour the mixture into tin. When cool, chill until set.
5. Remove the cake from the tin; remove foil.

Lemon Chicken Plait

Lemon adds zest to this ideal packed lunch recipe.

For 4 portions

Filling:
2 chicken joints
2 oz (50 g) button mushrooms
2 oz (50 g) margarine
2 oz (50 g) plain flour
½ pint (10 fl oz) milk
1 chicken stock cube
Rind and juice from ½ lemon
Salt and pepper

Pastry:
8 oz (200 g) plain flour
½ level teaspoon salt
4 oz (100 g) margarine
Beaten egg to glaze

1. Remove skin and flesh from chicken joints. Cut the flesh into small pieces; wipe and quarter mushrooms.
2. Melt the margarine in a medium-sized saucepan, add chicken pieces and mushrooms. Cook for 2 to 3 minutes until chicken has browned. Stir in flour, cook for 1 minute without browning. Remove from heat, add the milk and stock cube. Bring to boil, stirring, cook for 2 minutes.
3. Add the lemon rind and juice, season. Leave until cold.
4. Prepare a moderately hot oven (375°F, 190°C, Gas Mark 5). Lightly brush a baking sheet with melted fat.
5. Place the flour and salt in a bowl, add margarine and rub in until mixture resembles fine breadcrumbs. Add about 2 tablespoons cold water and mix with a fork to form a firm dough. Knead lightly on a floured board.
6. Roll out the pastry and trim to a 12 in square. Spread the chicken filling in a 4 in panel down centre of pastry. On each side cut pastry into ½ in strips.
7. Brush edges of strips with beaten egg. Fold strips alternately from each side across filling for plaited effect.
8. Place on to a baking sheet; brush with egg. Bake in centre of oven for 30 to 35 minutes until pastry is golden brown.

SLIMMERS

Monday

Two slices lean beef

Lemony apple and celery salad

Grapefruit segments

Tuesday

★ Creamy Pea Soup

Chicken breasts

Cottage cheese with pineapple

Wednesday

Liver and vegetable casserole

Cubed ginger melon

Thursday

★Ham and Celery Bake

Natural yogurt

Friday

☆ Egg mayonnaise

Cress salad

★ Plum and Apple Skimmer

★ see recipe opposite
☆ see daily notes

Note: Monday, Thursday and Friday can be accompanied by crispbread spread thinly with poly-unsaturated fat.

Creamy Pea Soup

Monday

Cut two thin slices of lean beef. Put on a paper plate and cover wth cling film. Peel, slice and core apple and mix with washed chopped celery; sprinkle with lemon juice. Put grapefruit in a sealed container. **Pack:** knife, spoon and fork, crispbread. **For tomorrow:** prepare Creamy Pea Soup. Cook the chicken.

Tuesday

Heat the soup and pour into a vacuum flask. Cut up chicken breasts. **Pack:** knife and fork. **For tomorrow:** cook the casserole for the family, reserving one portion in the fridge.

Wednesday

Pour the heated casserole into a wide-necked vacuum flask. Cube the melon and sprinkle with ground ginger. **Pack:** knife, fork and spoon. **For tomorrow:** make Ham and Celery Bake for the family, reserving one portion.

Thursday

Pack: knife, fork and spoon, crispbread. **For tomorrow:** hard boil an egg, wash and prepare cress for salad. Make Plum and Apple Skimmer for supper, reserving one portion.

Friday

Slice the hard-boiled egg and mix with low-calorie dressing. Take salad separately. **Pack:** knife, fork and spoon, crispbread.

Creamy Pea Soup

You can use a liquidiser to to make this warming soup.

For 2 portions

1 (5 oz, 142 g) can garden peas
2 rounded tablespoons dried skimmed milk
1 chicken extract cube
½ teaspoon Worcester sauce
Pepper

1. Press contents of can of peas through a sieve into a large saucepan. Mix together dried milk and 3 cans of water. Add to saucepan with chicken cube.
2. Bring to boil, stirring continuously. Add Worcester sauce and season to taste.

Ham and Celery Bake

When cold pack an individual portion in a plastic container.

For 4 portions

2 sticks celery
½ level teaspoon salt
1 oz (25 g) Cheddar cheese
4 slices cooked ham
English or French mustard
2 rounded tablespoons dried skimmed milk
1 egg
1 egg yolk
Pepper
1 teaspoon chopped parsley

1. Prepare a moderate oven (350°F, 180°C, Gas Mark 4). Pour ½ in water into a large, shallow roasting tin.
2. Cut 8 pieces of celery, each about 1½ in long. Cut remaining celery into ¼ in slices. Place celery in a small saucepan, with ½ pint (10 fl oz) water and salt. Bring to boil, cover and simmer for 5 minutes. Drain well, reserving liquor. Grate cheese.
3. Cut the ham slices in halves lengthwise, to make 8 long strips. Spread each strip lightly on one side with mustard. Place a 1½ in piece of celery on mustard on each slice; roll up firmly. Arrange rolls in a round, shallow, 1-pint ovenproof dish.
4. Make up ½ pint (10 fl oz) dried milk with reserved hot liquor. Beat egg and egg yolk together, stir in milk mixture and pepper. Pour into dish. Sprinkle grated cheese and remaining celery slices over egg mixture.
5. Place dish in roasting tin and bake in centre of oven for 25 to 30 minutes, until mixture has set and feels firm – remove dish from tin. Sprinkle with parsley.

Plum and Apple Skimmer

Pack an individual portion in a well-sealed container.

For 4 portions

¾ lb (350 g) cooking apples
½ lb (225 g) red plums
2 oz (50 g) dried skimmed milk
Liquid sweetener
1 egg white

1. Wash the apples and plums; cut into pieces. Place in a medium-sized saucepan, with 1 tablespoon water. Bring to boil, cover and cook for about 15 minutes, until fruit is soft.
2. Place the dried skimmed milk in a mixing bowl. Add 3 tablespoons water and beat with a wooden spoon until smooth. Using a wooden spoon, rub fruit through a nylon sieve into the milk mixture.
3. Mix well; leave to cool completely. Sweeten to taste.
4. Place egg white in a clean, grease-free basin; whisk until stiff, but not dry. Fold into fruit mixture. Turn out and chill.

Monday

Turkey salad

Cheesy peach halves

Tuesday

★ Cauliflower and Onion Soup

☆ Cold Spanish omelet with lettuce

Grapefruit and orange compote

Wednesday

★ Kidney Stew

Fresh fruit salad

Thursday

Celery cheese dip

Ham, gherkin and tomato wholemeal roll

Egg custard

Friday

Tuna with rice salad

Stewed rhubarb

★ see recipe opposite
☆ see daily notes

Note: Monday can be accompanied by crispbread spread thinly with poly-unsaturated fat

Cauliflower and Onion Soup

Monday

Dice up some turkey left from the Sunday roast, or use some cooked turkey pieces. Mix some tinned peach halves with low-fat cottage cheese. **Pack:** fork and spoon, crispbread. **For tomorrow;** make Cauliflower and Onion Soup and a hot Spanish omelet for the family, reserving enough for yourself for the next day. Prepare lettuce. Prepare a fresh grapefruit and orange and mix together.

Tuesday

Heat the soup and pour into a vacuum flask. Pack the cold Spanish omelet in a plastic container. Pack the lettuce separately. **Pack:** fork and spoon. **For tomorrow:** make the Kidney Stew for the family, reserving one portion. Prepare a fresh fruit salad with a little lemon juice and store in a container.

Wednesday

Heat the stew and pour into a wide-necked vacuum flask. **Pack:** knife, fork and spoon. **For tomorrow:** make a cheese dip, wash and chop the celery. Make an egg custard.

Thursday

Slice the ham and gherkin and tomato and make up the roll. Pack egg custard in a sealed container. **Pack:** spoon. **For tomorrow:** prepare a tuna and rice salad and stew rhubarb.

Friday

Pack: fork and spoon.

Cauliflower and Onion Soup

This can be packed into individual portions and frozen.

For 4 portions

½ lb (225 g) cauliflower (about half a large one)
2 small onions
1 teaspoon oil
1 chicken stock cube
Salt and pepper
¼ level teaspoon nutmeg
3 rounded tablespoons dried skimmed milk
1 egg

1. Wash the cauliflower; cut into small sprigs and chop stalk. Peel and finely chop onions.
2. Place the oil in a large saucepan, add onion and cook for 2 to 3 minutes. Stir in ½ pint (10 fl oz) water, stock cube, ½ level teaspoon salt, pepper and nutmeg. Bring to boil, stirring; add the cauliflower, cover and cook for 20 to 25 minutes, until cauliflower is tender.
3. Sieve soup (or liquidise in an electric blender). Rinse saucepan; return soup to saucepan, stirring.
4. Place skimmed milk in a measuring jug and make up to ¾ pint (15 fl oz) with water; add to saucepan. Beat egg and add to saucepan.
5. Stir over a moderate heat until slightly thickened (do not boil or soup will curdle). Taste and add more salt and pepper, if necessary.

Kidney Stew

Save an individual portion and pack in a wide-necked vacuum flask. Use the remainder for family supper, or you can make half the amount by halving the ingredients and keeping one portion in the fridge, for a day.

For 4 portions

1 lb (½ kg) onions
1 lb (½ kg) carrots
½ lb (225 g) turnips
1 lb (½ kg) ox kidney
½ level teaspoon mixed dried herbs
½ level teaspoon salt
Pepper
1 teaspoon Worcester sauce
1 beef stock cube
½ pint (10 fl oz) hot water
1 level tablespoon cornflour
Chopped parsley

1. Peel the vegetables. Slice the onions; cut carrots into ½ in slices; cut turnips into 1 in cubes.
2. Wash the kidney; remove skin and core and cut kidney into small pieces. Place onion in a large saucepan; place kidney on top. Sprinkle with herbs, salt, a shake of pepper and Worcester sauce. Add turnip and carrot.
3. Dissolve the stock cube in hot water; pour over vegetables. Bring to boil; reduce heat, cover and simmer for 50 minutes. Stir it once while it is cooking.
4. Place the cornflour in a basin and blend with 1 tablespoon cold water. Stir into liquid in saucepan; cook for 2 minutes. Taste and add more salt and pepper, if necessary, Sprinkle with chopped parsley before serving.

DRINKS

Hot drinks
These are not always 'on tap' at school or work. Prepare flasks of tea or coffee fresh every morning. On a chilly day, a more filling drink could be hot chocolate, cocoa or malted milk. For everyone, especially those who need warming, but are watching the calories, there are the meat or vegetable extract drinks. For small children, a vacuum flask with a glass inside is not the safest transport system – the glass could break if the flask is dropped. Try and buy instead, one of the new all-plastic ones.

Milk
This contains so much in the way of food value and is essential for growing children, or those doing hard physical work. Small or large cartons can be taken to work or school complete with a straw stuck on the outside with Sellotape, or a plastic cup. Add variety for children by making milk shakes. Pack them in a plastic beaker with a well-sealed lid.

Soft drinks
Fresh orange, apple, grapefruit, blackcurrant juices etc can be bought in small or large cartons. Stick a straw on to individual cartons. The larger cartons can be kept in the fridge and a suitable quantity be poured out daily into a plastic beaker with a well-sealed lid.

Canned drinks
There are so many kinds available that it's really a matter of laying in a stock of the ones that you or your family like best. Buy enough of the family favourites to last two or more weeks.

Home-made drinks
Some delicious and exciting drinks can be made surprisingly easily at home. These will ring the changes and supply nutrients. Slimmers, too, can ensure that the amount of sugar is controlled.

Strawberry Whisk

Makes 1 glass
Remove hulls from 4 strawberries; wash strawberries and place in a liquidiser goblet. Add ½ pint (10 fl oz) chilled milk and a few drops of pink food colouring. Run machine until mixture is smooth and frothy (or mash strawberries with a fork in a bowl; add remaining ingredients and whisk until smooth). Add sugar to taste.

Tomato Soda

Makes 1 glass
Place contents of 1 (4 fl oz) bottle tomato juice cocktail, 1 teaspoon Worcester sauce, pinch of salt and a pinch of dried sage into a large glass, mix well. Top up with soda water and ice cubes. Pour into a vacuum flask to keep cool.

Orange Tonic

Makes about 1¾ pints (35 fl oz)
Make up 1 (6¼ fl oz) can frozen orange juice as directed on can. Mix in 1 dessertspoon lime juice cordial and ½ pint (10 fl oz) ginger ale. Pack with ice cubes in a vacuum flask to keep cool.

Lemon and Orange Tango

Makes 1 pint (20 fl oz)
Scrub the rind of 1 lemon and 1 orange; cut fruit into 6 or 8 pieces and place in a liquidiser goblet with 4 oz (100 g) sugar and ¾ pint (15 fl oz) hot (not boiling) water. Run machine until mixture is well blended; strain and store in a screw-topped bottle in the fridge for up to 2 weeks. Dilute to taste. Pack with ice cubes in a vacuum flask to keep cool.

Grapefruit Tonic

Makes 2 glasses
Mix ½ pint (10 fl oz) chilled, unsweetened grapefruit juice with 1 (8½ fl oz) bottle of Indian tonic water in a jug. Wash a sprig of mint and add to the jug. Strain before pouring into a vacuum flask with ice cubes.

Vegetable Cocktail

For 2 glasses
2 sprigs of watercress
Half a stick of celery
2 tomatoes
Half a carrot
½ in piece of cucumber
Thin slice of peeled onion
1 level tablespoon tomato purée
Salt and pepper

1. Wash watercress, celery and tomatoes. Peel carrot; cut carrot, tomatoes, cucumber and onion into small pieces.
2. Place vegetables, tomato purée and ¼ pint (5 fl oz) of water in a liquidiser goblet and run machine until mixture is smooth.
3. Pour through a strainer into a jug. Taste: season with salt and pepper. Keep in the fridge.

Malted Milk Drink

Makes 1 glass
Place ½ pint (10 fl oz) milk and 1 level tablespoon malt and 1 level tablespoon malt extract in a saucepan over a moderate heat. Bring to boil, whisking. Pour into a heatproof glass and spinkle with ground nutmeg.

SAVOURIES

PUDDINGS, BISCUITS AND CAKES

RECIPES FOR SLIMMERS

Home made snack bars.

250 crunchy breakfast cereal
30 raisins
60 hazelnuts, roughly chopped
60 blanched almonds, chopped
45 plain wholemeal flour
45ml. veg oil
30 demerara sugar.
15ml. clear honey
1 large egg, beaten

greased shallow baking tin (30' x 18) and line. Place all ingredients and mix well. Spread in tin evenly and bake in pre-heated oven (mark 4) for 25 mins. Mark into 12 slices and allow to cool in tin